Integrating the ESL Standards Into Classroom Practice:
Grades 6-8

Suzanne Irujo, Editor

WRITERS

Barbara Agor

Roger Gee

Paula Merchant

Olga Ryzhikov

Susan Sillivan

Dorothy Taylor

Louise Young

Suzanne Irujo, Series Editor

 **TESOL** Teachers of English to Speakers of Other Languages, Inc.

Typeset in Optima with Dolphin display
by Capitol Communications Systems, Inc., Crofton, Maryland USA
and printed by Pantagraph Printing, Bloomington, Illinois USA

Teachers of English to Speakers of Other Languages, Inc.
700 South Washington Street, Suite 200
Alexandria, Virginia 22314 USA
Tel. 703-836-0774 • Fax 703-836-7864 • E-mail tesol@tesol.org • http://www.tesol.org/

Director of Communications and Marketing: Helen Kornblum
Managing Editor: Marilyn Kupetz
Additional Readers: Ellen Garshick and Christa Watters
Cover Design: Charles Akins and Ann Kammerer

ISBN 0-939791-86-2
Library of Congress Catalogue No. 00-130568

Contents

Acknowledgments

Thanks to the TESOL Standards Project Committee (Deborah Short, Nancy Cloud, Emily Gómez, Else Hamayan, Sarah Hudelson, and Jean Ramirez) for providing the solid foundation upon which the writers in this volume developed their units. The comprehensiveness and simplicity of the ESL standards facilitated our work.

Thanks to the TESOL Assessment Team (Anne Katz, Fred Genesee, Margo Gottlieb, and Margaret Malone) for developing a usable framework and procedures for assessing student achievement of the standards. Their work formed the basis of the assessment pieces of our units.

Thanks to Kathleen Graves, chair of the TESOL Publications Committee, for asking me to edit this volume and to serve as series editor. Working on these books has been very satisfying because of the importance of the project, and because it has brought me new friends and colleagues who have been a joy to work with.

Thanks to Marilyn Kupetz, Christa Watters, and Ellen Garshick for their editorial skills: Christa and Ellen for their keen eyes for details, and Marilyn for her knowledge, organizational abilities, patience, and warmth.

Thanks to the editors of the other three volumes in the series, Barbara Agor, Katharine Davies Samway, and Betty Ansin Smallwood, for their support throughout the process. Their insights, suggestions, and criticisms enriched my work.

And most of all, thanks to the writers of these units, Barbara Agor, Roger Gee, Paula Merchant, Olga Ryzhikov, Susan Sillivan, Dorothy Taylor, and Louise Young. Their enthusiasm for the project, punctuality in meeting deadlines, thoroughness in following the guidelines, and willingness to make yet another revision or supply yet another detail made my job as editor easy.

Series Editor's Preface

When I first saw a copy of *ESL Standards for Pre-K–12 Students* (TESOL, 1997), I thought, "These are very well done, but how are teachers going to use them?" Working with teachers since then, I've heard them echo those thoughts: "I really like these standards, but I'm not sure how to use them in my classroom."

The four volumes in the series *Integrating the ESL Standards Into Classroom Practice* are designed to help teachers use the standards. The series covers four sets of grade levels: pre-K–2, 3–5, 6–8, and 9–12. Each volume contains six units, some designed with a particular grade level or proficiency level in mind, others designed to span grade and proficiency levels. There are units for very specific contexts and units that are more general. All the units are adaptable for other levels and contexts and include suggestions for doing that.

These units were taught and written by real teachers, each of whom approaches the implementation of the ESL standards in the classroom in a different way. As I worked on editing the four volumes, I was struck by the wide variety of ways in which teachers who work with standards use them to inform their teaching. In describing what skills must be mastered by ESOL students in public schools, the standards become planning tools, observational aids, assessment guides, and ways of understanding language development.

These units also exemplify the strategies that Lachat (1999) recommends for teachers implementing standards-based instruction:

- Organize learning around what students need to know and be able to do

- Enrich their teaching by cultivating students' higher order thinking processes

- Guide student inquiry by posing real-life tasks that require reasoning and problem-solving

- Emphasize holistic concepts rather than fragmented units of information

- Provide a variety of opportunities for students to explore and confront concepts and situations over time

- Use multiple sources of information rather than a single text

- Work in interdisciplinary teams

- Use multiple forms of assessment to gather concrete evidence of student proficiencies (p. 13)

The teachers who prepared these units did so to demonstrate what they did when they taught the units, not to tell others what should be done. The units were designed to serve several purposes. We wanted them to be complete, finished products, usable as they are in other classrooms, so we made them as explicit as we could. We wanted them to be adaptable for use in other situations and contexts, so we included suggestions for doing that. We wanted them to serve as possible models for teachers who want to develop their own standards-based units, so we provided explanations for why we did things as we did.

These volumes expand upon and complement the work contained in previous TESOL standards publications. We have used appropriate descriptors and sample progress indicators as they appear for each standard in *ESL Standards for Pre-K–12 Students* (TESOL, 1997), although we have also created some new progress indicators when appropriate. We have tried to incorporate the assessment process outlined in *Managing the Assessment Process: A Framework for Measuring Student Attainment of the ESL Standards* (TESOL, 1998). Many of the checklists and rubrics used in the assessment sections are adaptations of those found in *Scenarios for ESL Standards-Based Assessment* (TESOL, in press).

A few technical notes:

- In keeping with the terminology used in *ESL Standards* (TESOL, 1997), we use *ESL* (English as a second language) to refer to the standards, the field, and our classes. We use *ESOL* (English to speakers of other languages) to refer to the learners themselves.

- In order to avoid having to repeat detailed procedures for teaching techniques that appear in several units in a volume, we have included a glossary of techniques. Because of this, there is no glossary of terms, but definitions of standards-related terms are available in *ESL Standards* (TESOL, 1997) and *Scenarios* (TESOL, in press).

- All resources and references for each unit are listed at the end of the unit. Writers annotated the resources where they felt it would be helpful to readers.

Our hope in producing these volumes is that teachers will be able to use these units in their own classes and that they will also gain insights into incorporating the ESL standards into other units they may develop. We want them to be able to say, after reading one or several units, "Now I know what to do with the ESL standards in my classroom."

Suzanne Irujo, Series Editor

REFERENCES

Lachat, M. A. (1999). *Standards, equity and cultural diversity.* Providence, RI: Northeast and Islands Regional Educational Laboratory at Brown University (LAB).

TESOL. (1997). *ESL standards for pre-K–12 students.* Alexandria, VA: Author.

TESOL. (1998). *Managing the assessment process: A framework for measuring student attainment of the ESL standards* (TESOL Professional Paper No. 5). Alexandria, VA: Author.

TESOL. (in press). *Scenarios for ESL standards-based assessment.* Alexandria, VA: Author.

Introduction

Many teachers and administrators in the field of ESL have mixed feelings about the movement toward standards-based education. We applaud the intention to promote higher achievement for all students. We recognize that standards can provide detailed descriptions of what our students are expected to achieve, thus facilitating our job of moving them into mainstream classes. We hope that the inclusion of ESOL students in standards-based assessment will help mainstream teachers and administrators realize that they, too, are responsible for our students' achievement.

However, if standards-based education is to achieve its aim of increased learning for all students, setting standards is not enough. Schools must provide the help that students need to achieve the standards. If they do not do this, our students will be tested for achievement of standards before their second language academic skills have developed to the point of being able to demonstrate that achievement in English. They will then be penalized for failing to do something for which they do not yet have the skills.

The ESL standards play a very important role in providing the help that our students need in order to meet standards. They provide the tools that ESL and mainstream teachers can use to ensure the success of ESOL students when they are included in mainstream standards-based assessment. To use the metaphor developed by the Standards Project team, they provide an "on-ramp" to the mainstream "highway" on which our ESOL students will have to drive (Cloud et al., 1997). They guide us as we develop programs and activities that will help our students achieve standards in content areas. They also give mainstream teachers who work with our students an understanding of what our students can do and what they should be moving toward. And they provide valuable ammunition to prevent our students from being penalized for not yet knowing enough English to achieve mainstream standards.

The ESL standards serve these functions at all grade levels, but guidance in navigating the on-ramp to the mainstream becomes especially crucial at the middle school level. As middle school ESOL students learn to use English to communicate in social settings (Goal 1), they are affected by the changes in language learning that occur around this age; they will need facilitation and focused practice to acquire correct conversational use of their second language. As they learn to use English to achieve academically in all content areas (Goal 2), they are affected by the fact that the complexity of the content area material they must learn increases greatly at this level. As they learn to use English in socially and culturally appropriate ways (Goal 3), they are affected, in both positive and negative ways, by the importance of the peer group.

The units in this volume present a variety of ways and contexts in which the ESL standards can be used. They are all content based because of the importance of content area learning in the middle school years, and Goal 2 standards are thus the most prominent. However, all the writers comment on how the ESL standards have helped them keep in mind the importance of language development in all areas, and Goals 1 and 3 are also fully represented.

A variety of content is represented in these units. Two social studies units deal with the Middle Ages and with communities "then and now." A science unit explores earthworms, and a science/mathematics unit develops measurement skills. A language arts unit teaches persuasive writing, and an interdisciplinary unit on the *Titanic* integrates science, social studies, and literature. All of the units have a very strong focus on language development.

We have tried to present a variety of contexts as well. We have units that were taught in ESL pullout classes, in self-contained ESL classes, in a sheltered content class, and in a mainstream class with ESL academic support. There are units for beginners/low intermediates, for intermediates, for high intermediate/advanced students, and for mixed proficiency levels. There are units for specific grade levels and for combinations of grade levels. In all cases, the units are readily adaptable for other contexts, and the writers offer suggestions for ways to do that.

In the first unit, Barbara Agor explores the theme of "Understanding Our Past" through a focus on the Middle Ages in Europe. Her writing highlights the fun of studying the Middle Ages with sixth-grade students, and she includes creative activities for introducing a topic that students may not be familiar with. The purpose of her unit is to give students a framework for studying any period of history, and her framework is easily adaptable to other historical periods. She also models a valuable way of looking at assessment as an ongoing strand within the unit.

Dorothy Taylor includes science, social studies, and literature in her integrated unit on the *Titanic*. In "Learning About Discovery and Exploration," students gain independent reading skills through intensive reading of a book about the *Titanic*. They also explore the scientific basis of underwater exploration and make connections to a previous social studies unit that focused on discovery. One of the highlights of this unit is the way in which Taylor designed her students' final projects in order to provide opportunities for individual students to develop the skills needed to meet particular standards.

Paula Merchant and Louise Young focus on "Investigating How Much" through a fantasy in which the "Keeper of the Erif" leads students through basic concepts of measurement. Their unit illustrates a team-teaching situation in which the ESOL students are an integral part of a middle school team, the science class is team-taught by a mainstream science teacher and the ESL teacher, and an ESL academic support class provides scaffolding to support what is done in the science class. This unit also includes some excellent suggestions for using the ESL standards for advocacy purposes.

The language arts unit written and taught by Susan Sillivan leads students through "Mastering the Art of Persuasion." The activities show how using content that students are familiar with (in this case radio, television, and print advertisements) can lead them to acquisition of new knowledge and skills. The unit also provides a model for combining the ESL standards with the English language arts standards of a particular school district in order to help ESOL students move from the shelter and support of the ESL class to the ability to independently attain standards expected in mainstream classes.

By "Exploring How We Live," Olga Ryzhikov helps students understand the concept of community and how a particular community has changed over time. Her unit focuses on colonial times and a present-day Maryland community, but the activities are adaptable for use with other communities. Her unit contains a very useful model for how to connect the social studies content of several different mainstream classes with the theme that students are studying in their ESL class.

Roger Gee guides his students through "Discovering the Interdependency of Living Things" in his unit on earthworms. He builds on the prior knowledge students acquired by encountering earthworms in the class garden and helps them understand a newspaper article on earthworms through modeling reading strategies in a read-aloud. He also turns the traditional teach/test sequence around, using a test as an introductory activity leading into independent research based on student-generated questions. His independent research model is one that can be applied in many other contexts.

We hope these units will serve as resources and models for teachers and administrators working to ensure that ESOL students benefit from the promise of standards-based education.

Suzanne Irujo, Editor

REFERENCE

Cloud, N., Gómez, E., Hamayan, E., Hudelson, S., Katz, A., Ramirez, J., & Short, D. (1997, March). *Helping experienced trainers and educators use ESL standards.* Workshop presented at the 31st Annual TESOL Convention, Orlando, FL.

UNIT 1
Understanding Our Past: The Middle Ages

BARBARA AGOR

Introduction: Why the Middle Ages?

> *An urban middle school hallway reveals the inner life of the school. What is that coming down the hall? It is deeply hooded, so we cannot quite tell what it is. It is ringing a bell! And what is it calling out? "Leper coming . . . leper coming."*
>
> *Some of its classmates shrink up against the walls, pulling their friends out of the way. Others dart out into its path, taunting, but always keeping a safe distance from the mysterious creature.*

Young adolescents can imagine themselves living in the Middle Ages. They see themselves as pages. They consider the possibility of being part of the Children's Crusade, worrying about where they are going and how they will find their way home. The study of the Middle Ages appeals to the middle school child's mind and spirit. The thought of lepers ringing bells to warn healthy people away captures their imaginations, as do the gory details of the bubonic plague, the prospect and purposes of torture, and the glory of dying for one's beliefs or one's true love.

The study of the Middle Ages appeals to me, too, as a teacher. Particularly at the middle school level, many attractive children's books provide powerful visual images, as well as thoughtful analyses. I like gathering these resources and seeing what new and beautiful books have been published since the last time I did the unit, and I like immersing myself, along with my students, in the subject.

Context

Grade level: Sixth grade

English proficiency levels: Mixed, from new arrivals to those with most of their schooling in English

Native languages of students: Spanish, Serbo-Croatian, Ukrainian, Laotian

Focus of instruction: ESL, social studies, language arts

Type of class: Pullout, 50 minutes daily

Length of unit: 5 weeks

Unit Overview

Our students need to know how to approach the study of history—what questions to ask, how to research historical topics, how to situate and represent what they have learned. For students whose formal academic knowledge is limited, I have found it useful to begin with a deep study of one historical period and then to extend the same approach—with activities they recognize immediately—to other historical periods as the school year progresses. Over the several years that we usually spend together, we acquire enough deep knowledge to consider themes across history and to address issues such as change, justice, systems, power, survival, and more.

In this unit, I introduce some of the key elements of the study of a historical period, using a favorite middle school topic, the Middle Ages, as an example. I hope that my students will be able to use the same scaffold, recognizing similar elements (e.g., time lines) as they study ancient Greece and Rome, the Colonial Period, the Civil War, the Depression, or any of the other usual middle school historical topics.

Thus my unit of study has two goals—content and process. The content goal is for students to become familiar with the kinds of information sixth graders should have about the Middle Ages. The process goal is for them to acquire enough basic knowledge, and to become comfortable enough with a variety of "ways in" to the study of history so that they begin to think across time periods to broader themes and issues.

This unit includes two strands that quickly interweave: Strand 1—uncovering knowledge—is the acquisition, processing, and provisional presentation of learning. This strand is largely, though not exclusively, content. Strand 2—assessment—is a more reflective, analytical one in which students plan, monitor, and formally present their work, and then assess it along with the work of their classmates. In Strand 2, we focus more on the process—learning how to learn, thinking about learning. The Middle Ages unit overview shows the organization of the two strands.

Unit Overview: The Middle Ages	
Strand 1: Uncovering Knowledge	**Strand 2: Assessment**
WHAT: Acquiring images and generating questions	
WHEN: Situating in time	
WHERE: Situating geographically	What are we learning?
HOW: The ways people lived	How do we know what good work looks like?
Further activities: WHO, WHY	Where do we go next? (How do we show what we know? Making provisional choices, planning the process)
	The final project presentation as social event
	The final project presentation as evaluation

And, no, I have not forgotten that I am teaching language. To the extent possible, I like to design activities that inevitably require certain grammatical structures. More often, however, the language on which we choose to focus emerges as a by-product of our work. Valuable language patterns spill opportunistically from the experience of inquiry and expression. We capture them as they pass.

When I plan a unit, I follow Wiggins and McTighe's (1998) advice to work backwards. I start by imagining what I want students to understand at the end of our study of the Middle Ages. Wiggins and McTighe contend that "the challenge is to point toward what is essential, not merely provide work that is entertaining" (p. 121). Although students have a great deal of choice in how they will present their knowledge and, indeed, which topics relating to the Middle Ages they will pursue, it is my job to identify several powerful essential questions or enduring understandings: issues that capture the essence of the Middle Ages and of historical study in general. This task is usually the most difficult part of my planning, but the most necessary, and sometimes the students help out.

This past year, the most powerful question came from Snježana, who asked, "Why are things different now? Why aren't we the same as the Middle Ages?" (Students' names in this unit are real and used with permission.)

Listening to Snježana, my three content goals became

1. Students will recognize that life in the past is not the same as life today and that life in the future will be different as well.

2. Students will understand that, even within the same historical period, people experience life differently, depending on factors such as gender, class, and so forth.

3. Students will know a lot of "stuff" about the Middle Ages.

In addition, there are two goals relating to process:

1. Students will articulate a process by which they can tackle the study of any historical period.

2. Students will continue to develop a disposition to evaluate—to give value to—their own and their classmates' work.

Toward the end of the unit, students develop final products, choosing from a variety of possibilities that, when completed, transform the room into a banquet of Middle Ages images and information. The walls speak through time lines, posters, maps, charts, graphs, and lists. A Jeopardy game in the corner focuses on facts, while addressing the eternal challenge of forming grammatically correct questions. Three-dimensional models crowd precious desktop space, while a TV screen displays a computer-generated slide show.

We conclude our work with various evaluations, distinguishing the content goals from the process goals. What is strictly about the Middle Ages? Which of the artifacts could remain on the walls as scaffolds, ready to be transferred to a new historical topic?

Standards

Having at least provisionally established the essential understandings, and having thought about how the unit will look at the end, I continue my planning. I look next—not necessarily in this order—at my resources, my interests, the interests of my students, and the relevant standards: *ESL Standards for Pre-K–12 Students* (TESOL, 1997) and New

York State's *Learning Standards for Social Studies* (University of the State of New York, 1996). Then I begin sketching my plans.

Many textbooks feature the Middle Ages as a unit of study. It is almost always part of the middle school curriculum. Because we have such rich print resources on the Middle Ages, it is a natural topic to use for developing parts of Goal 2, Standard 2: Use English to obtain, process, construct, and provide subject-matter information in spoken and written form.

In addition to content knowledge, this resource-rich topic also allows us to develop our students' ability to think, find meaning, and create a coherent product without having a full command of English. Here, we can incorporate Standard 3 of Goal 2: Use appropriate learning strategies to construct and apply academic knowledge.

I also use the ESL standards to show me what is missing. When I first designed this unit, it was clearly an academic (Goal 2) unit. And yet Goal 2 is only one of three major language areas identified by the ESL standards. Partly because of the strong focus on Goal 2, I decided to emphasize the social aspects of our final activity, addressing pieces of Goal 3: to use English in socially and culturally appropriate ways.

As I plan a unit, the ESL standards remind me of what my students need to be doing with language. For content and important subject-matter concepts, I rely on the New York State *Learning Standards for Social Studies*—in this case, Standard 2, World History.

> Standard 2, World History: Students will use a variety of intellectual skills to demonstrate their understanding of major ideas, eras, themes, developments, and turning points in world history and examine the broad sweep of history from a variety of perspectives.
>
> - The study of world history requires an understanding of world cultures and civilizations, including an analysis of important ideas, social and cultural values, beliefs, and traditions. This study also examines the human condition and the connections and interactions of people across time and space . . . .
>
> - Establishing timeframes . . . [and] examining themes across time and within cultures . . . help organize the study of world cultures and civilizations.
>
> - The skills of historical analysis include the ability to . . . explain the importance of historical evidence, and understand the concepts of change and continuity over time. (The University of the State of New York, 1996, pp. 12–13)

I also rely on standards as I assess my planning and teaching, and my students' learning and performance. The New York State standards remind me of the big picture when I get caught up in the gory details. The ESL standards remind me that language matters.

Activities, Strand 1: Uncovering Knowledge

To address Strand 1's task—the acquisition, processing, and provisional presentation of learning—we organize our inquiry around the *wh-* questions (who, what, why, where, when, how). This *wh-* question organization provides a cognitive scaffold that students can use to find and present information on any historical subject. It also moves them toward mastery of grammatically correct question forms.

Although I always start with the "what" activities, any of the other question words can follow.

What: Starting Out by Acquiring Images and Generating Questions

We are living in a world where images—television and movies—are often more powerful than the written or spoken word. Students are hungry for rich images in school, so I gather beautifully illustrated books and use them extensively. Every student, regardless of educational background, comes away from these activities with a visual sense of the Middle Ages, a provisional understanding of what it is all about. Almost all students generate questions that mean something to them. In other words, they are hooked.

> *Goal 2, Standard 3*   To use English to achieve academically in all content areas: Students will use appropriate learning strategies to construct and apply academic knowledge.
>
> ### *Descriptors*
> - focusing attention selectively
> - applying basic reading comprehension skills such as skimming, scanning, previewing, and reviewing text
> - formulating and asking questions
>
> ### *Progress Indicators*
> - scan several resources to locate potentially interesting images, topics, and information
> - generate questions relating to the Middle Ages and the study of history

PROCEDURE

- The book circle: I like to overwhelm students with print resources at the beginning of a unit. They are used to seeing 15–20 books propped up around the room. The books are there for several days before we begin the unit. Then, on the first day, the students move their desks into an approximate circle, and I bring out an egg timer. Each student starts with a book. They have 3 minutes to peruse it in any way that they want. One student is in charge of the egg timer and announces when the books need to move to the next person. If I have more books than students, I start to feed new books into the circle as all of the first set have been reviewed.

  Because the egg timer is always a desirable item, it seems unfair to leave it in the hands of one student. If the class can tolerate some disruption, I pair the timer with a specific book, and timer and book move around the circle. Handling the timer allows each student a few moments of distraction, and also allows each to be temporarily responsible for timing the exercise.

- Books and Post-its: The book circle is usually enough for the first day. On the second day, the library books come out again. I was so glad when

Post-it notes expanded their selection from washed-out yellow to the many colors they have today. Each student can have a particular color. Their task now is to take 5–10 Post-its and stick them on pages that they want to make sure their classmates see. Inevitably students include a picture of the martyrdom of Saint Apollinaire, in which she is tied to a board and held by her hair, with a faintly surprised look on her face, while a particularly dim-witted man extracts her teeth (Oakes & Biesty, 1989, p. 21). We conclude the second day's book circle by organizing our desks and chairs into two parallel lines (a **dyadic belt**) and students take turns telling a classmate about the Post-its in their books.

> It is easy to specify a language focus for talking about the books. I often suggest a beginning phrase, such as I like this because . . ., This is interesting because . . ., I think this means . . . because . . ., You should look at this because . . . .

- Graphic organizer: Now we have a collection of jumbled images and pieces of information. Our third and last introductory activity is to uncover what the class, as a group, has to say and, as their contributions emerge, try to shape them into categories. Most of my sixth graders have not had much experience creating graphic organizers, so we do this one together. Among the topics that are sure to emerge are knights and ladies, peasants, castles, religion, wars and weapons, disease, death, and, possibly, exploration. Cristina's graphic organizer (on p. 7) is typical.

> Making a graphic organizer together, with the various books open to the images, is a good way to involve beginning-level students. As they copy the teacher's diagram, or that of a fellow student, they can understand much of what they are writing from the pictures before them. Sometimes beginners add words in their first language as well.

- Questions: In addition to bits of knowledge, there will also be some good questions that emerge spontaneously, most coming within the first few days of study. Because I love the interest and autonomy that student-generated questions represent, I celebrate such questions. Usually I stop everything when someone raises a question. The students or I write these questions on a piece of newsprint that stays on a wall throughout the unit. Often we add the questioner's name to the question. Here are some examples:

  Whay do they fight all the time?

  Wher they rich?

> Sometimes the group will answer questions as fast as they raise them.
> - One student's question [on torture]: "Why don't they just kill them?" A classmate's answer: "To suffer more."
> - Another student's question: "How did they do the measuring?" A classmate's answer: "With a string. I know, because my mother told me."

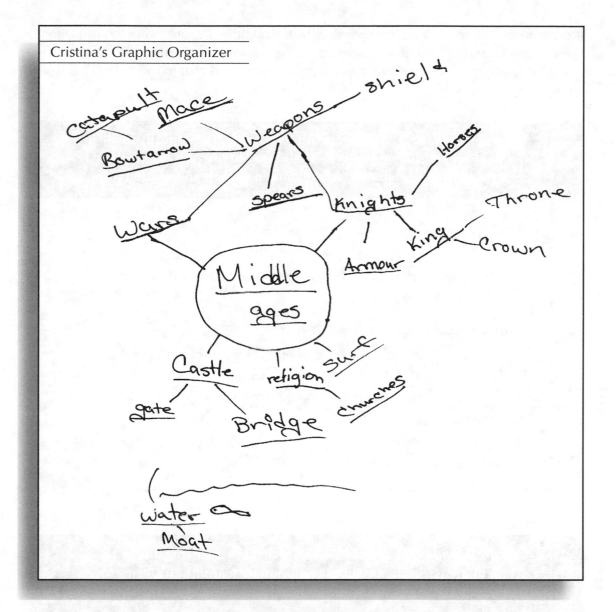

Cristina's Graphic Organizer

When did the Viking come?

How do people know what happened?

How do they get those big old rock on top of the catapult?

Why are things different now? Why aren't we the same as the Middle Ages?

Students' questions range from very concrete to highly sophisticated, and only a few lend themselves to clear answers in our books. One happy exception is the "how do we know" question, which is well addressed in many of the excellent resources listed at the end of this unit. In any case, these student-generated questions offer insights into students' thinking and confirm their role as makers of knowledge.

Where do we go next? Either the "when" or "where" activities can follow.

When: Situating in Time

I quickly realized that students needed a sense of time when one asked me, "When you lived in the Middle Ages, did you wear dresses like that?" To this day, I do not know if her question came from a confusion between *middle aged* and *Middle Ages,* or whether it came from a deeper confusion regarding historical time. Regardless of the cause for this misunderstanding, we now always do a time line fairly early in our study.

The following two standards apply to this activity, and also to the "where" and "how" activities described later.

Goal 2, Standard 2   To use English to achieve academically in all content areas: Students will use English to obtain, process, construct, and provide subject matter information in spoken and written form.

Descriptors

- selecting, connecting, and explaining information
- representing information visually and interpreting information presented visually

Progress Indicators

- construct a time line, noting beginning and ending dates of the historical period
- construct a map, showing important information
- make lists comparing Middle Ages to present times
- write a letter that shows awareness of differences between Middle Ages and present times

---

Goal 2, Standard 3   To use English to achieve academically in all content areas: Students will use appropriate learning strategies to construct and apply academic knowledge.

Descriptors

- focusing attention selectively
- actively connecting new information to information previously learned

Progress Indicators

- revisit student-constructed time lines periodically, adding new information
- take notes to summarize the main points provided in source material
- make lists, charts

PROCEDURE

- Time line models: We start by taking another look at the library book resources students have already perused. Almost every book will have a time line. What information does a time line represent? How? Are there different ways to represent this information? We take notes of the dates that appear to be important and interesting.

- Important events: We always start from the current year, encouraging students to recognize that time lines do have a relationship to a real time that they understand. Beyond that, we need to have a beginning and ending date for the Middle Ages. Students will quickly discover not only that information can be presented differently, but also that there is some difference of opinion about the information itself. The time lines in their books will give varying answers, which is a perfect occasion to talk about the arbitrariness of such historical periods and bring out the concept that people living in a certain age rarely recognize it as a distinctive time period, deserving of a name.

Students' first notes about interesting and important dates tend to be either wildly random or mindless copying. I have tried to focus attention by giving 10 pennies to each individual or small group. Then they might choose, for example, to give 5 cents to an event that they consider crucial, allocating their remaining 5 cents, a penny each, to five less important events. To provide further guidance, and to expand this activity into a simple mathematical exercise, we write the important events on the board and total up the money assigned to each.

Oakes and Biesty (1989) start their time chart in 343, with the Edict of Milan. Howarth (1993) starts her list of key dates with 410, the sack of Rome. What other beginning dates do students' books show? After entering the beginning dates, the same kind of conversation could take place about the ending dates (e.g., the capture of Granada and unification of Spain in 1492, or the death of Richard III in 1485).

- First draft: We start our rough draft with the current year (e.g., 2000), and then we add a beginning and an ending date for the Middle Ages. Students do not yet know enough to say for certain what the other significant dates might be, but some will be able to make suggestions and, because this is a draft, any date that they consider significant can certainly be included.

Because the mechanics of creating intervals and drawing and measuring lines can be a formidable task for some students, I prepare templates in advance for the students' first time lines. Another approach that eliminates the mechanics and helps students focus on the concepts is the software program TimeLiner (1994). Eventually, though, students do need to wrestle with the mechanics of computing intervals, measuring lines, and so forth.

- Revisions: As students acquire more information, they unfold their time line drafts and add dates and events. Eventually, one or more students may decide to do a more sophisticated time line as their project for the final presentation.

For some students, dates and the concept of time's passage are cognitively challenging. Extra support can include What year is it now? How old are you now? Use your fingers to count back 5 years: What year was it then? How old were you then? For homework, find out what year your parents, grandparents, aunts, and uncles were born. Practice the same concepts by making family time lines. Eventually, we can lead these students back to the idea that the Middle Ages occurred before anyone they know was alive. Even their teacher.

Where: Situating Geographically

Map study offers a particularly good way to meet the needs of a highly diverse class. I have often found that my not-yet-literate students have already acquired map skills and greatly appreciate the opportunities to show what they know and to build on that knowledge. A study of the changing representations of the world underlines how people's perceptions change, and how—in this case—exploration is affected by one's views of geography.

PROCEDURE

- Background knowledge: If students' social studies classes are progressing historically, they have probably already seen a good map of the Roman empire at its height, noticing how it extended through Europe, parts of Asia, and parts of Africa. If maps are not familiar to students, I locate some and remind students about ancient Rome and the fall of Rome. Keeping in mind that this unit is designed with a dual purpose—learning about the Middle Ages and learning how to learn history—it is useful to spend some time thinking about maps: What do you see in this map? Why is this map here? What is its purpose?

- Map models: Returning yet again to the resource books, students can look at the maps each author includes. Several books are likely to have maps of the silk route, which can be the beginning of many interesting conversations. Some books will have maps of the known world, showing only Europe, Africa, and Asia. This is an opportunity to further develop students' enduring understanding about change: Why did the Middle Ages' maps show only three continents? What needed to happen before people's knowledge of the world could expand?

- Geographical concepts: Many of my students have great difficulty differentiating between cities, states, countries, and continents. With several modern maps close at hand, they can look at medieval maps and develop those concepts while incidentally practicing useful language structures.

- Language practice: Comparing maps offers an opportunity to practice the formation of past tense questions:

  Did the people in the Middle Ages know about China? Yes, they did.

  Did they know about New York State? No, they didn't.

  Did they know about Egypt?

Did they know about France?

Did they know about Miami?

At a more advanced level, students can practice past tense statements in positive and negative forms:

They knew about China, but they didn't know about Florida.

They knew about Spain, but they didn't call it that.

- Index card game: After the grammatical forms become comfortable, this exercise can become a game. Students locate some familiar cities, states, and countries, write them on index cards, and use the cards as cues to elicit the questions and answers given above. As a teacher, I feel free to add a few locations of my own.

If some or all of the group can handle this level of complexity, we may talk about how names and borders have changed—Iberia in ancient Roman times, to modern-day Spain, for example. Such activities invite us again to look at the enduring understanding of historical change. What would cause national boundaries to shift? Have students in class experienced those changes of national boundaries in their own lives?

How: The Ways People Lived

After the first few *wh-* activities have begun, I often skip ahead to more planning and assessment activities (Strand 2), alerting students to where this unit will finally go. For clarity, however, I have added the remaining *wh-* activities here.

My students are always thinking about how people live, including themselves. I am constantly amazed and delighted by the extent to which they analyze their environment. Their enthusiastic powers of observation and interpretation are particularly evident to me when we are outside the classroom, at my home or on a trip into the suburbs.

As immigrants, refugees, or travelers to and from Puerto Rico, students do not have to stretch very far to be able to imagine another life—for example, the daily life of the Middle Ages. Many of the children's books on the Middle Ages attempt, with greater or lesser success, to answer the question, "How would you live if you were in the Middle Ages?"

A year-end visit to my house, 10 miles out of the central city, produced these observations:

Jaya: Aren't you afraid of the trees at night?

Josep: Where are all the people? No one's outside!

Carmen: I'd hate to live way out here. You're too far away from the police if you need them.

Picking up a carload of students for the year-end party produced this conversation:

Selma: Marla, you live in a bad neighborhood.

Marla: Yes, I do. But everyone knows my mother, so no one messes with us . . . I'm used to it.

PROCEDURE

- Two-column lists: Using pencil and paper or a two-column format on the computer, individuals or small groups list the characteristics of life in the Middle Ages and life today. Some students find it easier to start by enumerating what we do and have today. Others would rather pull out the books they have been using and start with the Middle Ages, as we see with Francisco's list.

  After the first draft of the lists, it is a good idea to have other students review them. This usually brings in some disagreement: "But we have stained glass now. It isn't just then."

- Letters to or from the Middle Ages: Now I invite students to write letters to a time traveler from the Middle Ages who will shortly arrive in our school. Or, if they prefer, they can become an adolescent from the Middle Ages who writes to us before we enter a time machine to go back in time. These letters can be great fun. They are also a form of evaluation, providing insights into the extent that

Some of my students find list making to be a linguistic or cognitive challenge. Usually they resolve the challenge by making a list of things we have today and then forming simple negatives: computers, no computers; markers, no markers; panty hose, no panty hose.

Having finished his letters of advice to a time traveler who was coming into the modern era from the Middle Ages, Francisco posed a question, "Would he want to go back?" Ivana, a refugee from Bosnia who has subsequently lived in several countries, replied poignantly, "Yes, he'd go back home. He's used to it there."

Francisco's List	
no cars	cars
weapons [spears]	guns
horse	horses
not alot of money	fan
tradeing	air conditioner
knights	phone
no medicen	electricity
no windose	clooks
castles	clean water
stained glass	radio
	plugs
	beter books
	pens
	planes
	elctronic games

Dear Jeffrey,

Things in the Middle Ages are not the way they used to be. Now we are having lots of wars. There are people who are dying because of the Black Death. All the knights are fighting with each other. The king is killing the people because they do not want to work for him.

Jeffrey if I was you I would not come. If you come bring some meidce for the Black Death.

individual students have been able to go beyond the relatively simplistic views of the Middle Ages they gained from television and movies to some deeper understandings. As with the lists, some students prefer to start with a letter from today, while others can jump right into the medieval mind. Artemio's and Snježana's letters show this (above and on p. 14, respectively).

A note about editing: I usually leave these letters as written. Some students will decide to make their letters part of the final presentation, and then, of course, further self- and peer-editing will occur.

Snježana's Letter

> Dear, ~~Kevin~~ Lilian
>
> I'm a girl from the 90's and my name is Snjezana you may think its a little wierd but it means Snowwhite now that you are coming to the 90's there are some things you definetly have to know about we have cure for black death but we have no cure for cancer but not many people get it and its not connunicable and we have make-up for eyes and lips all diferante colors and we have cars that ride on wheels instead of horses. There are much more new things you'll see. Good Luck,
>
> Sincerely,
> Snjezana

Further Activities

By now, the general direction of this work—organizing study by the use of *wh-* questions—should be relatively clear. Another place to go, as we continue to use question words, could be "Who: People and Roles." Activities for the last question word, *why?*, could range from the inevitable "Why do we have to learn this old stuff?" to deeply engaging questions. Sometimes these additional *wh-* questions go to students who can handle independent study.

Activities, Strand 2: Assessment

After perhaps three of the Strand 1 activities (what, where, and when), students have acquired enough knowledge to begin to imagine the final project. Their final project is to display in various ways what they come to know about the Middle Ages and to create a scaffold for future historical study. Through the activities thus far, they can imagine doing a time line and preparing a map. What other ways of demonstrating knowledge might they use?

After students have completed the Middle Ages unit, it will be easier for them to imagine the next similar final project, but this first project will take a great deal of time to conceptualize.

What Are We Learning?

Learning is built on prior knowledge. Most of my students are excited to reencounter something they learned before, particularly because many of them do not have a great deal of academic knowledge. Even those who are well schooled in several countries and several languages enjoy saying, "Oh yes, I learned about that when I was in [Germany/the camps/wherever]." Throughout our study, we look back and talk about what we have uncovered. We develop the habit of reviewing and elaborating on what we have already learned.

Goal 2, Standard 3 To use English to achieve academically in all content areas: Students will use appropriate learning strategies to construct and apply academic knowledge.

Descriptors

- actively connecting new information to information previously learned
- focusing attention selectively

Progress Indicators

- complete a form showing what is known so far about the Middle Ages, placing information in the correct columns
- categorize information
- modify information given by a peer

PROCEDURE

- What we know: Not-quite-pre- and not-quite-posttesting works very well for us. If I start a unit with "What do you know about the Middle Ages?", we get so little information that I have decided not to bother. Another unhappy consequence of such an open-ended question is that students without much school learning are once again brought face-to-face with their lack of knowledge and are overwhelmed by the competence of their classmates.

Students who cannot yet write can use pictures to show what they have learned, or they can "steal" words from those that are now up on the classroom walls. Often a literate student who is artistic chooses to draw rather than write, partly removing a possible stigma attached to not writing.

Instead, part way into the process, students enjoy making a two-column chart with one column headed, "What I knew before" and another "What I

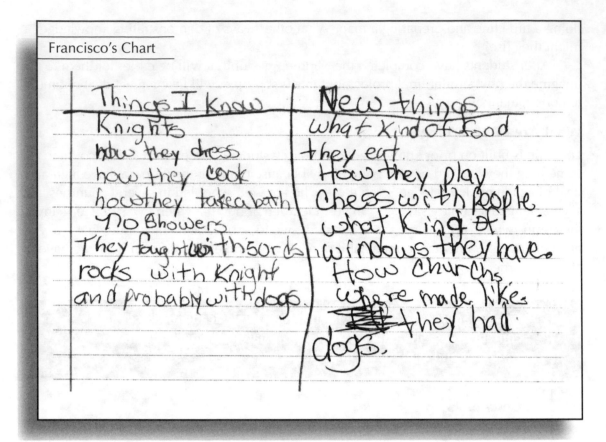

Francisco's Chart

Things I know	New things
Knights	what Kind of food
how they dress	they eat.
how they cook	How they play
how they take a bath	Chess with people.
No Showers	what Kind of
They fought with swords	windows they have.
rocks with Knight	How Churchs
and probably with dogs.	where made like
	they had
	dogs.

know now." I really do not care whether some new knowledge creeps into the "before" column, as it may have on Francisco's chart.

- Organization of our learning: As a follow-up to the two-column exercise above, we once again categorize our information, as we did with our first attempt at a graphic organizer. We revisit our rough and messy organizers, looking for categories that we all like, color-coding them, and then attaching the same codes to the ideas in our two columns. Here, as in most activities, it is perfectly fine for students to appropriate work of others, modifying and enriching their own first attempts.

- Achievement of goals: Chances are excellent that the concepts about change have become explicit by this point, but if they have not, I highlight the change/difference ideas that are implicit in the students' organization of knowledge and hope that this understanding carries over when it is time for them to develop titles for their presentations. Among the titles that could emerge are: "Different Lives, That Was Then . . . This Is Now."

How Do We Know What Good Work Looks Like?

This activity sets the stage for the final project evaluations and provides a structure for work in progress. Ideally, from now on, students will understand the criteria for success in whatever projects they choose to undertake.

Goal 2, Standard 3 To use English to achieve academically in all content areas: Students will use appropriate learning strategies to construct and apply academic knowledge.

Descriptors

- focusing attention selectively
- evaluating one's own success in a completed learning task

Progress Indicators

- develop a rubric that captures the key elements of a successful project
- apply the rubric for self- and peer-evaluation

PROCEDURE

- Time line rubric: At this point, the class will have enough knowledge about time lines to develop for them a rubric showing the characteristics of a very good time line (three points), an acceptable time line (two points), and a poor time line (one point). The class conversation is based on an examination of time lines from books, drafts of student time lines, and samples of good student work from previous years, if available. The finished product is shown in the time line rubric.

An enjoyable exercise that also develops language involves deciding, as a class, what terms we want to associate with a rubric score of 3, 2, and 1. Although yukky may be an accurate descriptor for a time line scoring a 1, students can develop a list of comparable words that convey value in a more formal way.

Time Line Rubric			
Score	**Dates**	**Appearance**	**Understanding**
3	At least 10 dates, including good beginning and end	Very neat Interesting letters and/or illustrations	Can explain why all dates are important
2	At least five dates, including good beginning and end	Some messy stuff, but I can read it	Can explain why at least half of the dates are important
1	Two dates or less	Looks like the writer didn't care (crumpled paper, many erasures)	Can't explain why more than one or two dates are important

- Self- and peer-evaluation: Now that the class has forged some agreement about what a good time line looks like, they revisit their earlier time line drafts, taking a day to see how much better they can do. Then they try their hands at assessing their own and one or two classmates' work. If, after their evaluations, they think that their rubrics need adjustment, they can do so.

- Map rubric: As individuals or in small groups, students can revisit their maps, as well as maps in the books they have reviewed, developing a rubric for maps in much the same way as they did for their time lines. Once this second rubric is created, and a class consensus reached, subsequent rubric development will be a comfortable, though still challenging, process.

Where Do We Go Next?

Now students know some things that they could do for their final projects, and they have a sense of how it will be evaluated. They know that their projects will be on display, and they know that not everyone can choose time lines and maps. Their work from now until the end of the unit is also good career education; they need to take what they know, decide what is important, figure out how to communicate in a way that is appropriate for their audience, identify the tasks associated with their final project, establish a time line for project completion, and monitor their progress.

Goal 2, Standard 1 To use English to achieve academically in all content areas: Students will use English to interact in the classroom.

Descriptors

- negotiating and managing interaction to accomplish tasks
- expressing likes, dislikes, and needs

Progress Indicators

- choose academic projects to complete individually or in small groups
- justify choices both in terms of personal interests and abilities, the wishes of classmates, and the need to comprehensively display subject-matter knowledge

Goal 2, Standard 2 To use English to achieve academically in all content areas: Students will use English to obtain, process, construct, and provide subject matter information in spoken and written form.

Descriptors

- persuading, arguing, negotiating, evaluating, and justifying
- selecting, connecting, and explaining information

Progress Indicators

- identify important knowledge about the Middle Ages
- determine how best to display that knowledge

PROCEDURE

- How to show what we know: A time line shows some information. A map tells different things. Now is a good time to review our print resources once again, and also pay special attention to a textbook, if available. How do our resources convey information? There are pictures, certainly, and words, as well as maps and time lines. What else? The Scott, Foresman series (Chamot, Cummins, Kessler, O'Malley, & Wong Fillmore, 1997, p. 83), for example, includes a very interesting list of a lord's daily activities.

Technology is a great leveler in an extremely heterogeneous class like mine. Students with very little written English who are also not very artistic can make an impressive presentation by importing images either from an on-line encyclopedia or a CD-ROM, or with a scanner. Several years ago, a patient and persistent twosome created a slide show using Kid Pix Studio (1994). They imported illuminated letters from an encyclopedia on a CD-ROM and scanned pictures from a calendar of the Middle Ages to make an alphabetical slide show. One screen, for example, would say, "C is for castle" and include a scanned picture of a castle. They did not complete the whole alphabet, but they received universal praise for their very attractive efforts.

- Provisional choices: In order to move on, students are now faced with a dual task—what to study further and how to present that knowledge. Usually, we talk about this as a group. By now, we have a sense of students' strengths. In fact, negotiations may occur in which an advanced-level student provides writing in exchange for a beginning-level student's illustrations.

  The hardest thing for my students to understand is that their choices truly are provisional. It is perfectly fine with me if they go partway into the work and decide they would rather do something else, or if they want to stay with the same topic but present it in a different way. (This option to change comes in very handy with students who sigh deeply and say, "This is boring!" I just tell them that if they choose to do something boring, that is their problem.) Even students who have worked with me for 3 years have trouble believing they truly can chuck it all and start somewhere else. Yet we change directions all the time in our out-of-school lives.

  There is no limit to the kinds of projects that students can select, including some that may not come to mind without some teacher prompting, such as the Jeopardy game that, once suggested, will always become a desired option. Another project, done at the very end, could be to create a list of questions that can be answered from the information displayed around the room. Many students will do more than one project—one associated with the content and another with the social aspects of the final presentation. We use a topic selection sheet, such as the one on the following page, to help make choices.

- Deadlines: An essential part of the flexibility of provisional choices, however, is deadlines. There has to be a "drop dead" point beyond which they have to make a choice and stay with it. We establish a schedule together, and we post it on a classroom wall. I also make individual

---

Topic Selection Sheet

Name _____ Date _____

1. I will start by finding out more about _____ .
   This interests me because _____
   _____ .

2. I want to show my information through _____ .
   This is a good way for me to show my information because _____
   _____ .

3. I want to work alone because _____ .
   or
   I will work with _____ because _____ .

4. I/We will look for information in the following sources: _____
   _____
   _____ .

5. Some things I/we already know about our topic are: _____
   _____
   _____
   _____ .

6. Some things we want to find out more about are: _____
   _____
   _____
   _____ .

---

checklists on attractive paper, so students can revisit their responsibilities from time to time and see how they are progressing.

- Communication throughout the process: This exercise is remarkably easy and useful. Every few days, we come together for about 10 minutes to check our progress against our deadlines, share what we are doing and learning, and talk about any problems we are having. After a certain point, this process becomes a friendly test. What is Nancy's project? What is Jasmin's? The ensuing awareness of others' projects helps counteract the single-minded focus of each student's project.

The Final Project Presentation as Social Event

Because my sixth graders receive ESL services in a pullout format, it is useful for their non-ESL classmates to have some sense of where their classmates go when they disappear. And because my classrooms over my career in five buildings have often been in a special education area (and because I do mainstream students who are clearly identified by others as special education), it is important for my students' classmates to understand that ESL is not a stigmatized class. The best way to accomplish these good purposes and to leave my students' non-ESL classmates with a sense of envy ("How do I get into this class?") is to invite them to join us as often as we can.

Goal 3, Standard 1 **To use English in socially and culturally appropriate ways: Students will use the appropriate language variety, register, and genre according to audience, purpose, and setting.**

Descriptors

- using the appropriate degree of formality with different audiences and settings
- recognizing and using standard English and vernacular dialects appropriately
- using a variety of writing styles appropriate for different audiences, purposes, and settings

Progress Indicators

- prepare written invitations for adults and classmates
- use telephone and leave telephone messages for adults and classmates
- advise peers on appropriate language use
- interact with an adult in a formal and informal setting

PROCEDURE

- Whom to invite: Inviting people to see our finished work helps students further develop their sense of audience. For this reason, it is preferable to start thinking about our final presentation before it is completed. Why do we want people to see our presentation? Who should see it?

- Invitations: Looking back over our list, how is the best way to invite each person? When should they come? What are the constraints on our invitees' time? What do we say in our invitations, and how do we say it? We want to practice both writing and speaking, recognizing in our language choices some differences in audience and in form.

- Follow up: Our invitees are no better or worse than people outside the school world. Some will respond promptly and graciously. Others never respond. What is appropriate follow-up? Sometimes we move from written invitations to spoken follow-up. Sometimes we go in the reverse direction. Occasionally we give up and, with much grumbling, cross someone off our list.

- Amenities: What refreshments do we want? Maybe a group will prepare something from one of the books that describes medieval food. This offers yet another opportunity for list making, as well as the mathematics of keeping our menu within budget.

The Final Project Presentation as Evaluation

After report cards have been received and opened, many of us teachers hear a student's accusatory complaint, "You only gave me a C." As do many teachers, I keep trying to convince students that it is not what I gave, but what they earned. By this point in our unit, students are used to assessing their own work and that of others. The following final assessment activities are simply an extension of a process they know well, one that they control to a very large extent.

Goal 2, Standard 2   To use English to achieve academically in all content areas: Students will use English to obtain, process, construct, and provide subject matter information in spoken and written form.

Descriptors

- responding to the work of peers and others
- representing information visually and interpreting information presented visually
- demonstrating knowledge through application in a variety of contexts

Progress Indicators

- create content-based questions relating to the Middle Ages, using information displayed around the room
- complete peer evaluations
- decide what parts of the Middle Ages exhibit (those representing process) stay for further study and what parts (those representing specific content) can be removed

---

Goal 2, Standard 3   To use English to achieve academically in all content areas: Students will use appropriate learning strategies to construct and apply academic knowledge.

Descriptors

- evaluating one's own success in a completed learning task
- planning how and when to use cognitive strategies and applying them appropriately to a learning task

Progress Indicators

- complete self-evaluations
- plan for future learning

PROCEDURE

- How I did, what I learned: The rubrics used throughout the project focus more on the quality of the work (how did I do?) than on content knowledge.

I have had very good luck with students looking over the assembled information and deciding, as individuals, as small groups, and as a class, what is worth knowing and how that knowledge could be represented on a test. Sometimes I remind them of the categories of our knowledge (our *wh-*questions), or remind them of a key issue—such as change or difference. I also ask them to devise some of each of what we call *fact* and *thinking* questions. I take their suggestions under advisement and create some kind of a test. They love recognizing their own questions in the final unit tests, and I rarely find that I have to use questions of my own.

- Next time: An important self-evaluation question, which students find difficult, is "What will I do differently the next time?" I ask this question as part of my continuing effort to undermine students' view that something done once is done right forever.

- Peer evaluation: I always ask students to fill out a peer evaluation sheet. At the beginning, students find it somewhat easier to evaluate their peers than they do themselves. Especially at this age, they can identify the malingerers

---

Peer Evaluation Sheet

Name_____ Date_____

1. The people in my group were _____
   _____ .

2. The best thing about my group was _____
   _____ .

3. If I could change one thing about the way my group worked, I would change _____ .

4. The person who worked the hardest was _____
   Evidence: _____
   _____ .

5. The person who did the least amount of work was _____
   Evidence: _____
   _____ .

6. I would like to say this about my work:_____
   _____ .

7. I (circle one)   would   would not   like to work with the same group again.

8. I would also like to say _____
   _____ .

in an instant and are brutally honest. As a teacher, I have many options for how to present these peer evaluations, and my presentation varies from student to student, depending on their degree of sensitivity. Usually I collect and edit the comments, and then give the student being assessed an opportunity to respond: *I agree/disagree because . . . .*

- Identification of the scaffold: Imagine that our next unit of study is the Blithrip Period, lasting from 1999 to 2599. How are we going to organize our inquiry? What pieces from our Middle Ages exhibition will we keep in the classroom to help us? What forms of presentation will help?

Additional Information

Because Strands 1 and 2 are so interwoven, I have included here a sample 5-week plan, showing how I go back and forth between the two strands (see p. 25).

RESOURCES

Resources for Students

For students, the number of books just keeps growing. Because this unit is designed to offer colleagues an outline for the study of history in general, almost all of the books included here are parts of larger series. Having used the ones below, I think that you will happily revisit other books in the same series as you deal with other historical topics.

Anno, M. (1980). *Anno's medieval world.* New York: Philomel Books.
> *This book highlights the intellectual history of the time, as well as the events that will be well known to the students, such as the Black Plague. It has very nice chronological notes in the back, beginning with the completion of the Parthenon in 432 B.C. and continuing to Armstrong and Aldrin's moon landing in 1969.* Anno's Medieval World *is not part of a historical series per se, but many students will recognize the author.*

Byam, M. (1988). *Arms & armor.* New York: Alfred A. Knopf.
> *The book is part of the extensive Eyewitness Books series. Students find the illustrations fascinating—pages and pages of swords, for example. One begins to see weaponry as art. Students who look only at the pictures will have trouble with the fact that not all the weapons were used in the Middle Ages. However, students who really want to study weaponry will profit by a review of dates and centuries (e.g., 550 is the 6th century) and will then have to pay attention to the brief explanatory texts, as well as the pictures, to make sure they are looking at weapons from the Middle Ages.*

Chamot, A. U., Cummins, J., Kessler, C., O'Malley, J. M., & Wong Fillmore, L. (1997). *ScottForesman ESL 7: Accelerated English language learning.* Glenview, IL: Scott, Foresman.
> *Although New York State puts the Middle Ages as part of the sixth-grade curriculum, this series locates it at the seventh-grade level. It is, however, equally interesting to both ages. There is as much illustration as text, and the colors are most inviting.*

Claire, J. D. (Ed.). (1993). *Fourteenth-century towns.* New York: Gulliver Books.
> *The illustrations in this book, part of the Living History series, are photographs of real models. Students like pictures that look real, though they sometimes have difficulty figuring out that the photographs are staged rather than authentic. The topics are naturally those that relate most directly to life in emerging towns, including markets, merchants and craftspeople, guilds, schools, betrothal and marriage ceremonies, several sections on the plague, and a great deal more. It ends with an excellent two-page chapter, "How Do We Know."*

Howarth, S. (1993). *The Middle Ages.* New York: Viking.
> *Like Catherine Oakes' book, this one is organized around topics. The topical organization makes it easy for students to compare information from several other sources on this list. Howarth presents more themes than Oakes, including such topics as pastimes, costume, and the family. In addition, there is a brief historical preface, "An Old Power Crumbles," which has easy-to-read and informative maps. The book also contains four transparent layers—not*

Five-Week Plan

Week #1	① WHAT — Book circle	① WHAT — Back to books – Post-its, Questions	① WHAT — Graphic organizers & Questions maybe Index	① WHEN — Timeline models imp. dates BCE/AD	① WHEN — Simple timeline
Week #2	① WHERE — maps mapgame	② WHAT I KNOW/KNEW + categories revisit graphic org.	② Rubric for timeline — self eval. of timeline	② Rubrics revisit — adjust — apply to peers create map rubric	② Talk about final project
Week #3	①/② WHAT'S WORTH KNOWING?	② How to represent knowledge	① How did people live?	① How write letters	② Develop content — make choices · establish deadlines
Week #4	② Review plans – start work	Research, produce, periodic progress checks			How close by Monday? Weekend homework needed?
		Plan/implement social components			
Week #5	Individual work for some Project layout for others — RSVP + nag	Start posting presentations. What needs to be done Wednesday?	Complete setting up for Thurs. — Review RSVPs, refreshments	② Presentation with guests	② Recover. Evaluate. Create scaffold which stays

① = Strand 1   ② = Strand 2

all equally valuable—showing interior and exterior views of a castle, a town street scene, a monastery, and a watermill. Regardless of my view of the transparencies' utility, students love the overlays and would probably enjoy using overhead projection transparency paper to create their own.

Macdonald, F. (1995). *How would you survive in the Middle Ages?* New York: Franklin Watts. Part of the *How Would You Survive?* series, this thoughtfully illustrated book opens with a time spiral beginning in 1352 B.C. and continuing through 1991. The narrative starts with,

"Begin your new life here," and is followed by 14 chapters, each addressing a specific question, such as *"Your home: Where would you live?" "Sports and games: How would you have fun?"*, and ending with *"Your history: How would you record your times?"* In an effort to acknowledge events of contemporary interest, the *"Timespan"* at the end of the book includes the Ottoman Turks' occupation of Serbia in 1389 and their capture of Bosnia in 1463.

Macdonald, F. (1997). *Marco Polo: A journey through China.* Danbury, CT: Franklin Watts.
This book is part of a new series, Exploration, which at this writing had only one other book, Magellan. Marco Polo captures the imagination of many of our students, who can see themselves as world travelers. It is full of fascinating little-known facts, such as Marco Polo's sighting of a black rhinoceros in Indonesia, which he decided was a unicorn. The book's illustrated description of silk-making was an eye-opener to my students, who had no idea that worms had anything to do with clothes they might wear.

Oakes, C., & Biesty, S. (1989). *The Middle Ages.* New York: Gulliver Books (Harcourt Brace imprint).
This book is the source of the St. Apollinaire illustration referred to in the first activity. It has lots of hand-drawn pictures. The text is presented in relatively brief chunks, and includes topics such as the arts and learning, religion, life of the nobility, life in the country, life in the towns, and exploration and invention. This book is part of the excellent Exploring the Past series.

Sibbet, E., Jr. (1980). *Cathedral stained glass coloring book.* New York: Dover.
It is always risky to be seen coloring ("Oh yes, the ESL class. That's where they color and have fun.") Nonetheless, students enjoy a Friday spent selecting a translucent panel and coloring with markers, and they come to understand what stained glass looks like. Sibbet and others have created several very attractive stained glass coloring books, all published by Dover. For students with problematic eye-hand coordination, the series includes small books of "stained glass" birds and animals that are considerably less intricate.

Some excellent student-constructed Web pages are available on the Internet, including the following:

Rice, A. (1994). *The Middle Ages.* Retrieved October 28, 1999 from the World Wide Web: http://www.byu.edu/ipt/projects/middleages/index.html.
Student-made Web pages on the Middle Ages come and go. When they can be found, they are often the best resources, because their language is closer to the language of our students. This site is a bit heavier on links than on student-written narrative, and some of the links have disappeared, but it remains a good and useful example.

Computer programs and Web pages that my students used during this unit include

The Annenberg/CPB Project. (1997). *The Middle Ages.* Retrieved October 28, 1999 from the World Wide Web: http://www.learner.org/exhibits/middleages/townlife.html.
This is probably the best single site, with links to all kinds of information. It uses the interactive media to good advantage. For example, there is a question box inserted into the text that asks the reader to name a cathedral that fell down. The reader follows links to pictures of four cathedrals, and then makes a guess, submits the answer, and is immediately told whether the answer is correct.

Castles Unlimited. (1999). *Castles of Britain.* Retrieved October 28, 1999 from the World Wide Web: http://www.castles-of-britain.com/.
Designed for students, this site has excellent pictures and a learning center that contains information that middle school students want to know (the privy, dungeons, medieval jobs). There are good bird's eye views of castles.

Kid Pix Studio [Computer software]. (1994). Novato, CA: Brøderbund.

TimeLiner 4.0 [Computer software]. (1994). Watertown, MA: Tom Snyder Productions.

Resources for Teachers

Because children's history books are so good, I use them almost exclusively as my own references. Two other sources are worth mentioning, however:

Manchester, W. (1993). *A world lit only by fire.* Boston: Little, Brown.
> *If you read only one adult book, read this. It provides a compelling, penetrating feel for life in the Middle Ages.*

Carlson, L. (1995). *Huzzah means hooray: Activities from the days of damsels, jesters, and blackbirds in a pie.* Chicago: Chicago Review Press.
> *Carlson's brief introduction is easy to read and not patronizing. Some of the book is appropriate for ages 3–9 (the dress-up section, for example), and the hands-on activities contain enough ideas for a decade of teaching. Her instructions for creating a castle (start saving toilet paper rolls now) work especially well, and the section on medieval games could become part of a classroom culture, with a life that extends far beyond the Middle Ages unit. Carlson has written other books in a similar mode. Also, there are several series by other writers that provide a similar hands-on approach to studying history.*

I always find something good on the Internet. Professors often post the content of their courses on-line, and I have encountered a number of interesting course syllabi including, recently, one with many links to other Internet sites relating to the Middle Ages. While the course syllabi often disappear from the Web after the completion of the course, the linked sites remain. Here is one of the most useful:

Georgetown University. (1999). *The labyrinth: Resources for medieval studies.* Retrieved October 28, 1999 from the World Wide Web: http://www.georgetown.edu/labyrinth/.
> *This is a classic reference, referred to by many other sites on the Middle Ages. It is perhaps of more use to teachers than students, though some pages, carefully selected, would be fascinating to students. The imagines are excellent, and (unlike some other Web pages) do not take too long to come up on the screen.*

Other Sources Cited

TESOL. (1997). *ESL standards for Pre-K–12 students.* Alexandria, VA: Author.

The University of the State of New York, State Education Department. (1996). *Learning standards for social studies.* Albany: Author.

Wiggins, G., & McTighe, J. (1998). *Understanding by design.* Alexandria, VA: ASCD.

UNIT 2
Learning About Discovery and Exploration: The Titanic

DOROTHY TAYLOR

Introduction

The hardest part about teaching a unit on the *Titanic* to my sixth graders was informing them that Leonardo DiCaprio would not be one of our guest speakers. Otherwise, engaging my students' interests in reading and studying about discovery and exploration, by reading Robert Ballard's (1993) book, *Finding the Titanic,* was quite easy, and I was not at all surprised when my group of sixth-grade beginning- and intermediate-level ESL students readily selected this book from a small collection I had given them.

We started this 5-week unit in the middle of February, that cold and dreary time of the year when nothing seems fresh anymore, and spring break is far away. But the classroom started to buzz the minute I raised Ballard's book in the air and began to give my short talk about it. "I've seen the movie 7 times," Sara exclaimed. "I saw 14," countered Teresa, "It make me cry." "That movie is real, Mrs. Taylor?" asked Alberto. "Of course it is," answered Mohammed. It was hardly necessary to take the customary vote to decide which book the majority of the class wanted to read. The vote was unanimous, and we were off on our own voyage of discovery.

Unit Overview

This class consisted of 13 sixth-graders pulled from four different mainstream classes. Their oral language ability ranged from high beginning to near-native fluency, and their reading levels ranged from pre-primer to about third-grade. In our school, the primary

---

Context

Grade level: Sixth grade

English proficiency levels: Beginning and intermediate

Native languages of students: Spanish, Korean, Arabic, Hindi, Creole, Chinese, Urdu

Focus of instruction: ESL/ language arts and science

Type of class: Pullout, 105 minutes daily

Length of unit: 5 weeks

---

role of the ESL teacher is to provide language arts instruction. However, I incorporate social studies or science into our curriculum whenever possible.

Because many of my students are not yet able to read independently, the units we study usually center around a book that we read together. Hence, choosing a book is an important process, and I feel that it is equally important that the students participate in its selection.

I included Ballard's (1993) *Finding the Titanic* in the selection of books to begin our new unit partly because of the popularity of the topic and the fact that it was written at a level I knew was appropriate for my students, but also because it dovetailed nicely with a prior unit on early exploration to the Americas. Much of the language and map work we had done in this earlier unit would help my students understand Ballard's book. The book also offered a rare combination of drama and science that allowed for interesting teaching possibilities.

Once the students made their final selection, I mapped out a series of activities, shown in the unit overview, to explore the literary and scientific sides of the book.

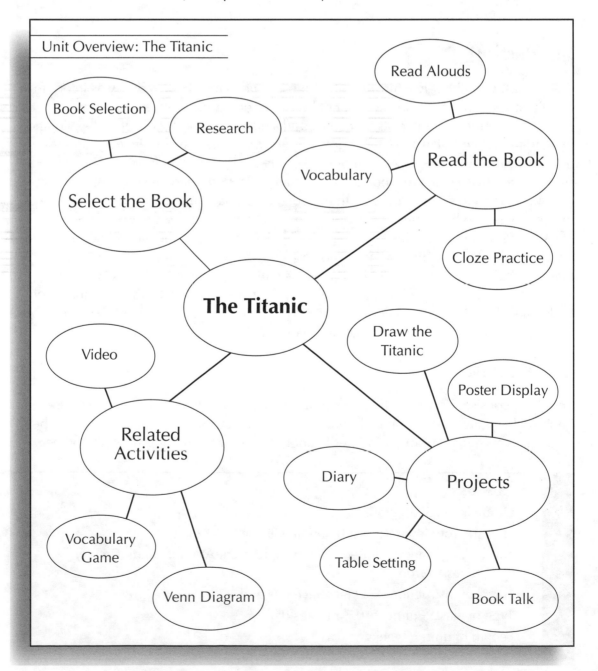

Unit Overview: The Titanic

Standards

As I developed my plans for this unit, I had two broad objectives in mind: to help my students further understand the concept of exploration, and to help them improve their reading ability. *ESL Standards for Pre-K–12 Students* (TESOL, 1997) guided me beyond these two academic objectives to a more comprehensive view of my students' needs. One of the benefits of the ESL standards is that they have allowed me to adopt a broader view of students as I consider the three goals of personal, academic, and social uses of English. At the same time they have led me to narrow and focus my planning more effectively through use of the descriptors and progress indicators.

Students enter my classroom with a variety of educational backgrounds and language abilities. Each student is working toward the same standards but may need a particular combination of activities, strategies, or techniques to reach those standards. I used the descriptors as a resource to tailor my activities to meet individual students' needs. At the same time, descriptors yielded progress indicators that gave me an important assessment tool.

As I planned my lessons for this unit, I considered how each activity would help my students meet the standards, and never more so than when developing the options for the final project. I carefully read through each of the goals and standards, trying to include choices from more than one goal or standard. Although I did not think I needed to include every goal and every standard in one unit, I did want my students to have as many means as possible to display their knowledge. I think that one advantage of the ESL standards is the diversity of ways to meet and assess those standards. As my students developed and modified their final projects, their approaches to work and learning made me realize how many ways there are to meet and assess standards. I suspect that as my students and I continue to explore ways of navigating the standards, our discoveries will be every bit as valuable as those from the *Titanic*.

Introductory Activities

Book Selection

My group of typical preadolescent sixth graders had strong feelings about everything. The pressures that many of them felt in their mainstream classes and at home were enormous, and they were quick to reject any idea or ruling presented by an adult. One successful compromise that we negotiated early in the year was that they would be involved in decisions about what we would read in class. As our unit on Martin Luther King was drawing to a close, the speculative buzz about what we would be reading next began. I followed the process that I had used in previous selection of reading topics, which was to gather a group of five or six books from which to choose one to read together. The grouping in this unit was heavily loaded with science and fiction books because these were genres that we had not yet read this year.

PROCEDURE

- I presented the five or six books that the students could select for the unit by giving a short talk about each book. I read the summary on the back, if there was one, and answered any questions. After I presented the books, I passed them around for the students to look at and discuss. While they were looking at the books, I wrote the titles of the books on the chalkboard.

> **Goal 1, Standard 1**   To use English to communicate in social settings: Students will use English to participate in social interaction.
>
> ### Descriptors
>
> - expressing needs, feelings, and ideas
> - getting personal needs met
> - engaging in conversations
> - conducting transactions
>
> ### Progress Indicators
>
> - ask peers for their opinions, preferences, and desires
> - engage listener's attention verbally and nonverbally
> - elicit information and ask clarification questions
> - indicate interests, opinions, or preferences related to class projects
> - negotiate solutions to problems, interpersonal understandings, and disputes

- I answered additional questions from the students after they had looked at the books, and allowed about 15 more minutes for discussion. (Often these discussions would become quite heated as small clusters of students lobbied for certain books; however, in this instance, the *Titanic* book was so popular that most of the discussion centered around the movie, as students competed to show how much they knew.)

- I held up each book and gave a short reminder of what the book was about as a student monitor took the vote and wrote the numbers on the board. In this case the vote was unanimous for *Finding the Titanic.*

ASSESSMENT

I used an observation note sheet to assess students' use of English during the discussion about the books. As I developed this observation sheet, I was guided by a similar one included in TESOL's (in press) *Scenarios for ESL Standards-Based Assessment.* The categories observed were taken from the progress indicators for this activity.

Research

As much as I owed to the movie *Titanic* as a motivating factor, I knew that one difficulty with this topic would be distinguishing between the fact and the fiction of the movie itself. Before beginning our book, we began an ongoing **K-W-L chart**. As I expected, many of the initial questions and comments were concerned more with the characters of the movie than with the realities of the true *Titanic.* However, as we continued to discuss the fiction of the story line as opposed to

> I made notes of comments about the books to use in planning future units. For example, I noted that some of the students said that one book was "too easy" and "for little kids." When I asked them why they thought so, they told me that the print was too large and the pictures were silly. I decided to keep both of these factors in mind when selecting books for our next unit.

the reality of the tragedy, we moved further and further away from the movie and into a more realistic quest for information.

Goal 2, Standard 2 To use English to achieve academically in all content areas: Students will use English to obtain, process, construct, and provide subject matter information in spoken and written form.

Descriptors

- listening to, speaking, reading, and writing about subject matter information
- gathering information orally and in writing
- selecting, connecting, and explaining information
- representing information visually
- formulating and asking questions

Progress Indicators

- synthesize, analyze, and evaluate information
- research information on academic topics from multiple sources
- construct a chart synthesizing information
- locate reference materials
- gather and organize the appropriate materials needed to complete a task

PROCEDURE

- I reminded the students that we were going to be reading a book by the man who searched for and discovered the *Titanic* at the bottom of the ocean. In small groups of two or three I gave them a K-W-L chart and asked them to fill in the "What I Know" and "What I Want to Learn" sections of the chart.

- The small groups shared their information with the whole class. We consolidated the information and filled in a large K-W-L chart that grew and stayed in front of the classroom throughout the unit.

- Each week a different pair of students was assigned to find the answers to the questions in the "What I Want to Learn" section of the chart. They used the first 15 minutes of the class that were normally devoted to individualized reading to do so. Sometimes they could find the answers in the book we were reading. At other times, they

Because the reading ability of the class was so diverse, I always included as wide a range of reading levels as possible when I gathered book collections. By doing so, I was able to challenge experienced readers while not frustrating novice readers.

referred to a small collection of books that I had gathered on the subject, or to the Internet, where I had bookmarked several sites about the *Titanic,* ships, and exploration. I generally paired more fluent readers with emergent readers, but they still needed a good deal of teacher guidance to complete this task.

- The assigned pair wrote the answers to the questions on their small K-W-L charts. I reviewed and edited them for spelling and grammar, and they then completed the large K-W-L chart. A sample chart follows.

K-W-L Chart for the *Titanic*

What I Know	What I Want To Learn	What I Learned	How I Learned It
The Titanic sank.			
Many people died.			
The captain died			
Some people lived.			
It hit an iceberg.			
	Were Jack and Rose really on the Titanic?	No. They were not real people.	Internet: Jeremy Skarr's Titanic Page
	How many people died?	1,518 people died	Internet: *R.M.S. Titanic*
	How big was it?	It had 9 decks and it was as tall as an 11-story building.	*Finding the Titanic* by Robert D. Ballard
	How did they get water?	They used water maker machines to take salt out of the ocean water.	Internet: *Sailing Thru Science*
	Where did it sink?	Close to Newfoundland, Canada Latitude 40° 44′ N Longitude 49° 55′ W	Internet: *Titanic: Raising a Legend Exploring the Titanic* by Robert D. Ballard
	How many people lived?	705	Internet: *R.M.S. Titanic*
	How many lifeboats did it have?	20 lifeboats	*Drawing the Titanic* by Andrew Staiano

- Each Friday, the assigned pair presented the information they had obtained to the whole class and added three or four more questions to the W section of the K-W-L chart.

ASSESSMENT

I kept a checklist of students who had completed this task each week. In addition, the two students who were assigned to do the research for the week completed self-assessment checklists at the end of their research week. This checklist was adapted from one found in *Scenarios for ESL Standards-Based Assessment* (TESOL, in press). On their self-assessment checklist the pair noted if they were able to answer the questions for that week and if they worked well with their partners. Occasionally, students would complain that their partner dominated the computer or that they felt they had done most of the work. I noted these in my records but also discussed with the students ways of resolving such differences.

> When I organize students in small groups or pairs, I take many factors (academic and personal) into consideration. For the K-W-L activity, I tried to group fluent speakers with emergent speakers. However, for the weekly research work I paired fluent readers with emergent readers and computer-savvy students with computer novices.

On their checklist the students included where they got the information to answer the questions from the K-W-L chart. After the first week we began to add these references to our class K-W-L chart. In addition, I used this information to see which reference materials the students were using the most. The Internet, not surprisingly, was the most popular. The students and I continued to add sites during the unit as I discovered that students were willing to struggle much harder to read something on the Internet than from a book. Books with many pictures were the second most popular resource.

Book Reading Activities

The reading level of the students in this class ranged from pre-primer to third-grade. Most were reading at a first- or second-grade level. A few of the students were highly literate in their native language and were transferring those skills into English. However, the majority of the students in the class came from backgrounds with little education. Lacking the reading skills and vocabulary necessary to decipher a printed text, most of the students were understandably reluctant readers.

One of my major goals for the school year was to help these students become independent readers. However, reading is a task that involves many different cognitive functions. The actual reading of the book *Finding the Titanic* (Ballard, 1993) was another ongoing daily unit activity that incorporated a variety of minilessons and subordinate exercises in order to help my students develop these cognitive functions. Each subordinate activity had its own goals and standards, and I will describe them briefly below.

Daily Read Alouds

Although there are many opponents of this old-fashioned activity, I found that short doses of reading aloud allowed us to focus on specific strategies as a group and within a specific context.

Goal 2, Standard 3   To use English to achieve academically in all content areas: Students will use appropriate learning strategies to construct and apply academic knowledge.

Descriptors

- focusing attention selectively
- applying basic reading comprehension skills such as skimming, scanning, previewing, and reviewing text
- using context to construct meaning

Progress Indicators

- use verbal and nonverbal cues to know when to pay attention
- verbalize relationships between new information and information previously learned in another setting
- rehearse and visualize information

PROCEDURE

- We devoted about 15 minutes of each day to reading aloud. I never forced a student to read aloud; rather than resisting the activity, students clamored and bid for their turn to read.

- As students read aloud, I made few corrections. I had also trained the class to give struggling readers ample time to figure out a word themselves rather than providing the word for them.

- One reading strategy we focused on during our read alouds was understanding prefixes and suffixes. For example, when Pratha stumbled over the word *unsinkable,* I wrote the word on the board, breaking it into its three parts *(un-sink-able).* I proceeded with a spontaneous minilesson on the prefix *un-* and suffix *-able,* explaining the meaning with words and pictures.

Mrs. Taylor:	(underlining *sink*) We've already talked about this word. It means to go under water. (I draw a picture of a ship underwater.) This part of the word (underlining *able*) is called a *suffix.* It gives you more information. Does anyone want to tell me what *able* means?
Jae Lee:	You can do something. I able read.
Mrs. Taylor:	That's right. I'm able to read. I can read. So what does *sinkable* mean?
Alberto:	It can sink.
Mrs. Taylor:	Exactly. Now let's look at this part (underlining *un*). The part of the word that comes at the beginning is called a *prefix.* It has a meaning, too. Does anybody know what it is? (Silence) What if I said, "You are unable to go

outside for recess today because it is raining." What does *unable* mean?

Mohammed:	We can't go outside.
Mrs. Taylor:	Right. *Un-* means no or not. So what does *unsinkable* mean?
Several students:	It can't sink.
Mrs. Taylor:	Right. (Quoting from book) "Some people even said the ship was unsinkable" (p. 5). It wasn't able to sink (drawing a picture with ship on top of water and an *X* over the picture of the sunken ship).

ASSESSMENT

As students read aloud I kept a modified **running reading record** in a notebook. A sample of what this record looks like is shown. I used my running records to develop minilessons in reading strategies, such as phonics, recognizing words within context, and vocabulary development.

Vocabulary

Vocabulary acquisition is a constant, ongoing task for beginning- and intermediate-level language learners. In order to ensure that students knew the meaning of the important words from the book, I prepared a vocabulary worksheet for each chapter.

Modified Running Record

NAME *Diego*

BOOK *Finding the Titanic*

Date, page no.	Miscues	Notes
2/26 p.7	began—begin rescue—res— wondered	found ✓ ok our past tense
3/2 p.15	wouldn't — won't seeing though - th— sight- si—	M.L. silent *gh*

In my records I note miscues, particularly patterns, such as leaving off endings. However, in my "notes," I also record areas of strength. For example, after Diego finished reading his paragraph on page 7, I complimented him on his ability to pronounce the [au] dipthong in *found* and *our*. On March 2, the *M.L. silent gh* refers to the mini-lesson on the silent *gh* that Diego's difficulties with *though and sight* prompted.

Goal 1, Standard 3 To use English to communicate in social settings: Students will use learning strategies to extend their communicative competence.

Descriptors

- exploring alternative ways of saying things
- learning and using language chunks

Progress Indicators

- use written sources to discover or check information
- test appropriate use of new vocabulary, phrases, and structures
- associate realia or diagrams with written labels to learn vocabulary and construct meaning

PROCEDURE

- For each chapter in the book, the students completed a vocabulary worksheet on which they wrote in their own words the meaning of the key words that we had discussed in that chapter.
- Where possible, if they chose, they could also draw a picture that indicated they understood the word.

ASSESSMENT

For many of our discrete-point worksheets, I used a system of checks to evaluate the student's work. Students who demonstrated an understanding of 80% or higher received a check plus. Students who demonstrated an understanding between 70 and 80% received a check. Students whose work showed that they understood less than 70% of the assignment received a check minus, and I met with them individually to review the material. Students who did not complete the work received a zero for that assignment and made arrangements with me to make up the work. For the students, it was a simple way to measure their work. I used this information, along with running reading records, portfolios, and anecdotal records, when I assigned grades and in conferences with parents. I also noted patterns in understanding and misunderstanding for future lessons.

Cloze Reading Practice

Cloze reading passages are included in the language arts section of the *Standards of Learning* (Commonwealth of Virginia Board of Education, 1995) recently implemented in our state. In addition, sixth-grade ESL students are given the *Degrees of Reading Power* (Touchstone Applied Science Associations, 1989), a cloze-based test, as part of their assessment for placement into middle school. These tests replace random word deletions with a more systematic focus on a specific strategy for reading in context. While we were studying the *Titanic,* I gave three separate minilessons on strategies for taking cloze tests. I used the information and vocabulary from our reading to develop lessons and subsequent practice worksheets that focused on three strategies for successfully using context clues to complete fill-in-the-blank or multiple-choice, cloze-type exercises. The three strategies I focused on were

1. recognizing antonyms and antonym cue words, such as *but* and *however*
2. using time-order words to correctly complete a sequence
3. identifying and matching pronoun referents

Goal 2, Standard 3 To use English to achieve academically in all content areas: Students will use appropriate learning strategies to construct and apply academic knowledge.

Descriptors

- focusing attention selectively
- applying basic reading comprehension skills such as skimming, scanning, previewing, and reviewing text
- using context to construct meaning
- applying self-monitoring and self-corrective strategies to build and expand a knowledge base

Progress Indicators

- use antonyms, time-order words, and pronoun referents to complete cloze exercises
- verbalize relationships between new information and information previously learned in another setting

---

PROCEDURE

- I explained to the students the importance of cloze-based exercises to future tests that they would be taking. I then gave a minilesson on the topic. For example, I explained that antonyms were opposites, demonstrating orally and with gestures *up* and *down, under* and *over* and giving students opportunities to guess and give other examples of antonyms.

- The students completed three or four examples from a worksheet in class and finished the worksheet for homework. We reviewed the worksheet the next day and discussed questions or difficulties they had.

ASSESSMENT

I collected at least one of each type of worksheet and used the check system explained above to record the results in the student's record. I also used these worksheets to observe patterns of under-standing and misunderstanding. However,

When the class was working independently, I helped students who were having difficulty with exercises such as these. For example, students spent the first 15 minutes of each class reading books of their choosing. During this time, I would take students who were having difficulty with the cloze procedure to a conference table, and we would review the lesson. As we went over the worksheet, I would ask the students to explain how they selected their answers. These explanations often helped me understand the students' thinking processes. I used this information to guide our review lesson.

Sample Cloze Exercises on Antonyms

When they left the docks in England the water was calm, but when the *Titanic* sank, the water was _____.

    a. tranquil
    b. green
    c. numb
    d. rough

Most of the women and children survived the sinking of the *Titanic,* but many of the men _____.

    a. drowned
    b. drifted
    c. hurried
    d. sat

---

a more thorough assessment was conducted through class discussions as I encouraged the students to reflect out loud on problems or misunderstandings that they encountered. With continued practice and discussions, all the students were able to complete these worksheets with at least 80% accuracy.

Other Activities

Vocabulary Picture Game

All eyes are on Rebecca as she selects a small slip of paper from the box that the teacher holds.

Mrs. Taylor: *Do you know what it means?*

Rebecca   *(smiling as she looks at the word): Easy.*

Sara: *You so lucky.*

Juan: *C'mon Rebecca, you can do it.*

With pressures for students to do well on standardized tests and survive academically in the mainstream classroom, I often find myself losing sight of the social and cultural needs of my ESL students. My students tell me that they seldom speak in their mainstream classrooms because they are afraid of "sounding stupid" to the native-English-speaking children in the class.

The ostensible purpose of the vocabulary picture game that we played every Friday was to review the new words we had studied that week. However, a much more important goal of the game was to give the students an opportunity to interact with each other in ways that more formal lessons do not accommodate.

Goal 3, Standard 3 To use English in socially and culturally appropriate ways: Students will use appropriate learning strategies to extend their sociolinguistic and sociocultural competence.

Descriptors

- observing and modeling how others speak and behave in a particular situation or setting
- experimenting with variations of language in social and academic settings
- analyzing the social context to determine appropriate language use
- deciding when use of slang is appropriate

Progress Indicators

- observe language use and behaviors of peers in different settings
- rehearse different ways of speaking according to the formality of the setting
- test appropriate use of newly acquired gestures and language

PROCEDURE

- Every Friday I wrote each of the words we had studied that week from our reading on a small piece of paper.
- The students divided themselves into two teams. After flipping a coin to see which team went first, the first team member selected a slip of paper and then drew a picture of that word on the chalkboard.
- The other members of that team had 1 minute to guess what the word was. If they guessed correctly, they received a point. If they did not guess correctly, the opposing team had 15 seconds to guess the word and receive a point. If neither team guessed the word, the team member drawing the picture told the class what the word was and explained the meaning of the word.
- Team members continued taking turns back and forth between the teams until all of the words had been selected.

ASSESSMENT

As the students played the game, I made a note of words they had difficulty with and reviewed those words with the class at the end of the game or the next Monday. I also logged in students' anecdotal records any noteworthy observations on how they conducted themselves in socially or culturally appropriate ways.

Venn Diagram

The story line in Ballard's (1993) book moves back and forth in time between 1912, when the *Titanic* made its voyage, and 1985, when Ballard discovered the shipwreck. As we read the book, some of the research questions on our K-W-L chart were technical ones about why the *Titanic* sank. As we gathered information through our reading and research, I asked the students to complete a **Venn diagram** comparing the technology that the captain and crew of the *Titanic* used with the technology used by Ballard in his search for the wreck.

Goal 2, Standard 2   To use English to achieve academically in all content areas: Students will use English to obtain, process, construct, and provide subject matter information in spoken and written form.

Descriptors

- comparing and contrasting information
- gathering information orally and in writing
- selecting, connecting, and explaining information
- listening to, speaking, reading, and writing about subject matter information
- representing information visually

Progress Indicators

- locate information appropriate to an assignment in text or reference materials
- construct a chart synthesizing information

PROCEDURE

- I led a whole-class discussion on the differences between technology in 1912 and 1985.

- Using a large chart, I explained how Venn diagrams worked, and together we filled in some differences and similarities between technology used in 1912 and 1985. In pairs, students filled in a smaller diagram.

- As a group, we discussed the findings of the pairs and completed the large chart, as shown in the Venn diagram illustration.

- The next day I reviewed the Venn diagram and gave a minilesson on writing a compare and contrast essay. On a large piece of chart paper, I displayed the shell of a four-paragraph compare and contrast essay. Beside each paragraph I wrote a descriptor: "Introduction," "1912," "1985," and "Conclusion." After explaining the purpose of each of these paragraphs, I elicited sample sentences from the students that I used to fill in the shell.

Students with learning disabilities (LD) often have difficulty copying work from the board. If the work to be copied comes from a large chart or overhead transparency, I often take down the chart or transparency after the other students are finished copying it and let the LD students take it to a quieter corner of the room. If the work comes from my notes, I simply give the students my original notes to copy from.

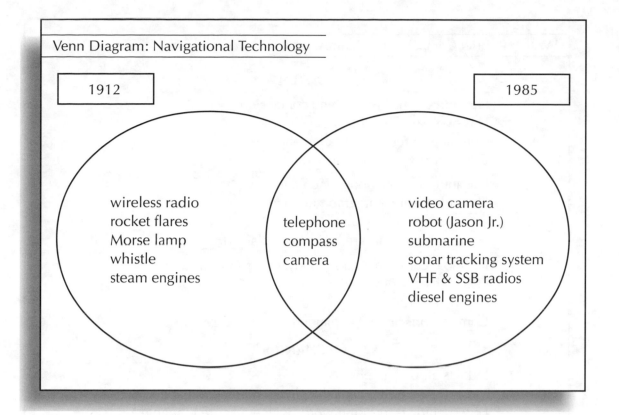

Venn Diagram: Navigational Technology

| 1912 | | 1985 |

1912
wireless radio
rocket flares
Morse lamp
whistle
steam engines

(overlap)
telephone
compass
camera

1985
video camera
robot (Jason Jr.)
submarine
sonar tracking system
VHF & SSB radios
diesel engines

- Homework: The students completed a compare and contrast essay using the information from their Venn diagrams.

ASSESSMENT

I was able to assess and adjust the group's understanding of the Venn diagram during our whole-group discussion. I walked around as the students worked in pairs and made notes that I used to clarify and explain during our second whole-group instruction. I used the writing rubric shown on page 44 to assess the student's compare and contrast essays.

Watching a Video

The students lounged in front of the television, munching popcorn and drinking soda.

Jesenia: *Is that Mr. Robert in that shirt with stripes?*

Prathi: *Look, Jason [the robot] from the book!*

Claudette: *When they gonna find the* Titanic?

Watching the video was one of the culminating activities for this unit. The video *Secrets of the Titanic* (Noxon & Ballard, 1986) about Ballard's search for and discovery of the *Titanic* closely followed the book that we had read. The students responded enthusiastically as they were able to experience visually the book they had just finished reading.

Writing Rubric: Compare and Contrast Essay

CONTENT

√+	Has introduction, body, *and* conclusion Has two-paragraph body Compares three or more elements Comparisons are logically explained
√	Has introduction, body, *or* conclusion Has at least one paragraph in body Compares two elements Some comparisons are logically explained
√–	Has no clear introduction, body, or conclusion Has no clear body Compares one or no elements Comparisons are not explained

MECHANICS

√+	Indents all paragraphs Most sentences are capitalized with correct punctuation Few spelling errors, and words with errors are readable
√	Indents some paragraphs Some sentences are capitalized with correct punctuation Some spelling errors, and a few words with errors are unreadable
√–	Does not indent paragraphs Few sentences are capitalized with correct punctuation Many spelling errors, and words with errors are unreadable

PROCEDURE

- We treated this activity as a celebratory one, so I allowed students to bring snacks and drinks to class. Because we had just finished reading the book, little introduction was necessary.

- The students viewed the film, asking questions and making comments as we watched. Occasionally, but not often, I would pause or rewind the video to answer a question or point out an object or dialogue of particular interest. The students especially enjoyed the shots of the interior of the ship and often called out when they spotted parts of the ship that we had studied.

When I have beginning-level speakers in my classes, I often encourage them to display their knowledge with pictures when they do not have the words to do so.

> **Goal 1, Standard 2**   To use English to communicate in social settings: Students will interact in, through, and with spoken and written English for personal expression and enjoyment.
>
> ### Descriptors
>
> - describing, reading about, or participating in a favorite activity
> - expressing personal needs, feelings, and ideas
>
> ### Progress Indicators
>
> - listen to, watch, and respond to a video
> - recount events of interest

- After watching the video all students had an opportunity to tell what impressed them the most about it.
- For homework, the students wrote or drew pictures of their favorite part of the video. A few students volunteered to share their writing and drawing the next day.

ASSESSMENT

As the students watched the video, I made notes of any questions and comments and used those notes to clarify any misunderstandings or invite comments after we had watched the video. The students received a check if their assignment demonstrated an understanding of the video, and a check plus if they volunteered to share their completed assignment with the class.

Final Projects

Many of the activities for this unit were conducted in lessons involving the class as a whole, but I also wanted to give the students an opportunity to produce a piece of work that was geared toward their individual interests, strengths, and talents. In addition, I knew that the final projects needed to allow for the great differences in oral and reading and writing abilities among the students.

As we made our way through the Ballard book, many possibilities for projects emerged. About midway through the book, I presented the students with several options. The students selected and worked on these projects during class time and at home for the final 2 weeks of the unit and presented them to the class in the final week of the unit. Because the students worked on their projects during class and at home, it is difficult to know how much time they spent on them, and I am also sure that the times varied. However, I estimate that students spent 1–2 hours preparing their final projects. Each presentation lasted 5–10 minutes. The final projects option list is shown on page 46, and the following activities represent the projects that the students elected.

Draw and Label the *Titanic*

The students who chose this project used Ballard's (1993) book and other resource books to draw a picture of the *Titanic* and label the parts of the boat from vocabulary that we had learned previously.

Final Projects Options List: The *Titanic*

Below is a list of projects you can choose for your final project on the *Titanic*. You can do your final project by yourself or with one or two partners. Next week, I want you to tell me what your project will be and if you will be working with a partner. Your project must be finished by MARCH 19. You will present your project to the rest of the class.

1. Draw the *Titanic* and label the important parts *(bow, stern, deck, cabin, hull, crow's nest, anchors, lifeboats, passengers, crew, captain)*.

2. Make a map showing where the *Titanic* departed, where it sank, where the survivors were picked up, and where the Titanic was going.

3. Make a poster showing the technology that Robert Ballard used to find the *Titanic (Alvin, Jason Jr., video cameras, underwater sled)* and explain how each was used.

4. Make a poster showing the objects that Robert Ballard found *(pots and pans, cups and saucers, bathtubs, staircases)*.

5. Prepare a book talk on *Finding the Titanic*. Be sure to include the title and author. Choose a favorite part of the book to read and tell whether you would recommend it to a friend and why.

6. Make a table setting showing what kind of dishes and silverware you might have seen in the first-class dining room of the *Titanic*.

7. Write a *Titanic* diary. Pretend you are one of the passengers on the *Titanic* and write a diary as if you were onboard the ship.

8. Make a crossword puzzle. Use important words from the *Titanic* and write clues for those words.

9. Choose your own project. You can make up your own project.

IMPORTANT DATES:

NEXT WEEK: TELL ME WHAT YOUR PROJECT IS AND WHO YOU ARE WORKING WITH

MARCH 19: FINISH YOUR PROJECT

MARCH 22–26: PRESENT YOUR PROJECTS

PROCEDURE

- Prior to presenting their drawings to the class, the students rehearsed the pronunciation of the words with a peer.
- They then presented the information to the class by showing the drawing as they pointed to the labels and read the words. The illustration shows one student's drawing.

> **Goal 1, Standard 3**   To use English to communicate in social settings: Students will use learning strategies to extend their communicative competence.

Descriptors

- selecting different media to help understand language
- practicing new language

Progress Indicators

- test appropriate use of new vocabulary, phrases, and structures
- associate realia or diagrams with written labels to learn vocabulary or construct meaning

Poster Display

Although my explanation of the poster project was purposefully loose, three students worked together on this project to create quite an impressive display. They made a three-paneled poster, with each panel explaining a different aspect of Ballard's exploration and discovery of the *Titanic.* Each student worked on one panel. Each panel contained pictures with short explanatory captions underneath. The first panel showed a map of the *Titanic*'s voyage and where it sank. The second panel showed the equipment that Ballard used to find the *Titanic.* The third panel showed some of the relics that Ballard found while exploring the sunken ship.

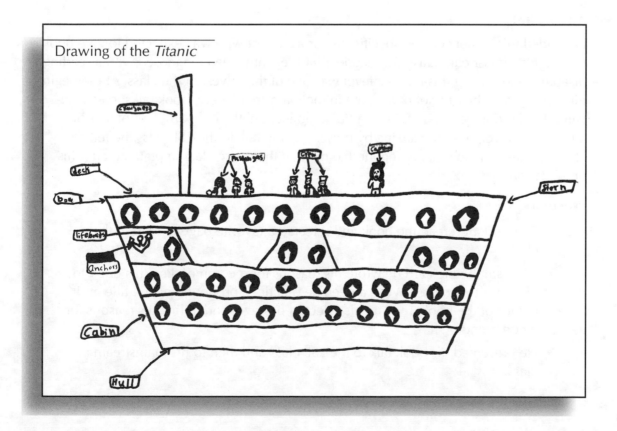

Drawing of the *Titanic*

Goal 2, Standard 3 **To use English to achieve academically in all content areas: Students will use appropriate learning strategies to construct and apply academic knowledge.**

Descriptors

- planning how and when to use cognitive strategies and applying them appropriately to a learning task
- recognizing the need for, and seeking, appropriate assistance from others (e.g., teachers, peers, specialists, community members)

Progress Indicators

- make pictures to check comprehension of a story or process
- select materials from school resource collections to complete a project
- rehearse and visualize information

PROCEDURE

- The students discussed what they would present in their poster and divided the work into three areas. They assembled the materials they would need for their panels from the Internet, magazines, or by drawing the pictures, and wrote short sentences to go with each picture. After the students edited one another's sentences, I also edited them.
- The students then assembled the pictures and the sentences on the display panels. In their presentation, they explained their own panels to the class.

A Book Talk

I included this project option specifically for a student who was expected to give book talks in his mainstream class. This student had recently been diagnosed with a reading disability and, in fact, his reading level was one of the lowest in the class. At the beginning of the year, he did not participate in the mainstream class book talks, partly because he did not feel ready to read a book independently and partly out of fear of failure. However, after rehearsing by presenting the talk to the ESL class, he felt ready. His mainstream teacher later reported to me that the entire class applauded after his presentation.

PROCEDURE

- The student reread the book and selected a favorite page to read to the class.
- On a small note card he wrote his reasons for recommending this book to his mainstream class. With a peer, he practiced pronouncing the title and author of the book, reading his selected passage, and telling his reasons for recommending it.
- He presented his book talk to the ESL class and then to his mainstream class.

> **Goal 1, Standard 2** To use English to communicate in social settings: Students will interact in, through, and with spoken and written English for personal expression and enjoyment.
>
> **Descriptors**
>
> - describing, reading about, or participating in a favorite activity
> - expressing personal needs, feelings, and ideas
>
> **Progress Indicators**
>
> - recommend a game, book, or computer program
> - listen to, read, watch, and respond to plays, films, stories, books, songs, poems, computer programs, and magazines

A *Titanic* Table Setting

Many of the students were fascinated by the grandeur of the dining room from the movie, drawings in the book, and pictures from the wreck. We had spent time discussing what *china* and *silverware* were, and two girls who were at a high beginning level chose to bring these words to life by recreating a table setting from the *Titanic*'s first-class dining room and enacting a dinner conversation between two of the characters in the book we had read.

> **Goal 3, Standard 3** To use English in socially and culturally appropriate ways: Students will use appropriate learning strategies to extend their sociolinguistic and sociocultural competence.
>
> **Descriptors**
>
> - observing and modeling how others speak and behave in a particular situation or setting
> - rehearsing variations of language use in different social and academic settings
> - analyzing the social context to determine appropriate language use
>
> **Progress Indicators**
>
> - model behavior and language use of others in different situations and settings
> - rehearse different ways of speaking according to the formality of the setting

PROCEDURE

- The girls researched an appropriate table setting for the first-class dining room by watching the movie and looking at pictures in books. They gathered the appropriate items for a place setting by begging and borrowing them from their homes and acquaintances. They rehearsed their oral explanation of the table setting with me.

- They also prepared an oral drama of a conversation between two passengers on the *Titanic* and rehearsed that conversation with me.
- They presented an explanation of the table setting and their drama to the class.

A *Titanic* Diary

Three girls who enjoyed writing each chose to write a diary as if they were one of the passengers on the *Titanic*. Not surprisingly, each of the three girls chose to write as if she were Ruth Becker, a 12-year-old survivor of the tragedy who was featured in the book we read in class.

> **Goal 2, Standard 2**   To use English to achieve academically in all content areas: Students will use English to obtain, process, construct, and provide subject matter in spoken and written form.
>
> ### *Descriptors*
>
> - retelling information
> - selecting, connecting, and explaining information
> - representing information visually and interpreting information presented visually
> - demonstrating knowledge through application in a variety of contexts
>
> ### *Progress Indicators*
>
> - read a story and represent the sequence of events (through pictures, words, music, or drama)
> - edit and revise own written assignments
> - use contextual clues

PROCEDURE

- The girls reread the book to determine what key information they should include in the diaries.
- They each wrote a first draft of the diary, discussed the first draft with a peer and revised, and then gave me a copy of the second draft. I made some content and editing suggestions. They then wrote final drafts of their diaries and prepared pictures to go with them.
- They presented their diaries to the class by reading them and showing the pictures. An excerpt from one girl's diary is shown on page 51.

An Excerpt From *Titanic* Diary

Today morning, me and my mom went to Cafetaria I wish my dad is here. my brother was busy to run around with his new friends. After I ate my breakfast, I went to deck, this ship has fance around, so we won't fall. I like to see fresh see and smell. Suddenly, I got little tears on my eyes. because the sea remineds me that I played with my friends in England that we played closed to sea. I spent most time on the deck today. and I felt so sad today for no reason. End.

Final Assessment

After handing out the final project options, we brainstormed, as a whole group, ways of evaluating the projects. Afterwards, I organized their ideas and made up the checklist shown below, which was completed by the student giving the presentation, by other students in the class, and by me.

As we moved through our unit on the *Titanic,* I used my ongoing assessment to plan and revise my day-to-day lessons. Although I developed each of the checklists and

Final Project Checklist: The *Titanic*

Date _____

Your Name _____

Presenter's Name _____

About The Presentation	Yes	Sometimes	No	Comments
Spoke loud enough to be understood				
Spoke clearly enough to be understood				
Looked at audience				
Used new words we learned				
Used clear pictures or props				
Told where information came from				
Writing was readable				
All partners participated*				
About the Audience				
Listened carefully				
Didn't talk or interrupt				
Asked questions				

*Only check if there is more than one presenter

What I liked best about the presentation: _____

_____

_____

_____

rubrics to fit the needs of these particular students and this specific unit, I was continually guided by two texts. The first was *Assessing,* one volume in a series called *Expanding Expectations Language Resource Guide* (Fowler & McCallum, 1998), a language arts resource guide produced by Fairfax County Public Schools. The other was TESOL's (in press) *Scenarios for ESL Standards-Based Assessment.*

At the end of the unit, I conducted a more thorough evaluation. To evaluate individual students, I assembled the assessment tools that I had used: running reading records, anecdotal records, rubrics, checklists, and completed worksheets. I used this information to complete report cards and to share with the students' mainstream teacher and parents during conferences. This step corresponded to the third and fourth stages of the assessment process outlined in TESOL's (1998) *Managing the Assessment Process.*

In addition to assessing individual students' progress and needs, I looked for patterns of development and need within the group as a whole to determine what direction our future lessons should take. Here again, the ESL standards guided me as I noted which standards our unit on the *Titanic* had not addressed and made plans to incorporate them into the next unit's activities.

Conclusion

In the end, the *Titanic* proved to be a successful unit. It was one in which the students were heavily invested. They chose it because of the popularity of the subject. However, popularity and interest alone are not measures of learning. For me, the growth that the students exhibited through evidence of the progress indicators within the standards was a valid and measurable record of the unit's success. Of course, it would have been more successful if Leonardo DiCaprio had been a guest speaker.

REFERENCES AND RESOURCES

Books

Bailey, D. (1990). *Ships*. Austin, TX: Steck-Vaughn.
> *This book tells the history of ships, including steamships and ocean liners. It is fairly easy to read.*

Ballard, R. D. (1993). *Finding the Titanic*. Toronto, Canada: Madison Press Books.
> *This book was written by one of the scientists who discovered the* Titanic *shipwreck. It provides an easy-to-read account of the sinking of the* Titanic *and Ballard's efforts to discover the shipwreck. The drawings and photographs are clear and striking supplements to the text. We used this book as our main text throughout the unit.*

Ballard, R. D. (1988). *Exploring the Titanic*. Toronto, Canada: Madison Press Books.
> *The text of this book is much more sophisticated than Ballard's* Finding the Titanic, *but it also contains more details about both the ship and its discovery and many more drawings and photographs.*

Graham, I. (1993). *Boats, ships, submarines and other floating machines*. New York: Kingfisher Books.
> *This book explains why ships float and what instruments they use. It is easy to read and has colorful illustrations.*

Kentley, E. (1992). *Boat*. New York: Albert A. Knopf.
> *A colorfully illustrated book that includes the history of ships and shipbuilding,* Boat *has pictures of many types of ships and their inner workings.*

Lord, W. (1955). *A night to remember*. New York: Bantam Books.
> *The author of this book is one of the most well-known chroniclers of the* Titanic. *The book gives a step-by-step story of what happened the night the ship sank.*

Lynch. D., & Marschall, K. (1992). *Titanic: An illustrated history*. Toronto, Canada: Madison Press Books.
> *This book combines many photographs and illustrations of the* Titanic *with an easy-to read text.*

Marschall, K. (1997). *Inside the Titanic*. Boston: Little, Brown.
> *Containing cutaway illustrations of specific sections of the* Titanic, *this book also has a four-page foldout of the ship.*

Scholastic. (1996). *Boats and ships*. Toronto, Canada: Author.
> *This book contains colorful graphics, transparent pages, and stickers. It contains a great deal of information about ships, including explorers, ocean liners, and navigational instruments.*

Staiano, A. (1998). *Draw the Titanic*. Lake Mary, FL: Tangerine Press.
> *This book gives easy to follow instructions for drawing the* Titanic, *its captain, lifeboats, and other important components of the ship. It also has information about the* Titanic, *including interesting facts, presented in attractive boxes, throughout the book.*

Video

Noxon, N., & Ballard, R. (Producers and Directors). (1986). *Secrets of the Titanic* [Video]. (Available from National Geographic Society, PO Box 98199, Washington, DC 20090-8199)
> *This video shows Ballard and his crew using underwater cameras and robots in the search for and discovery of the* Titanic. *Because it closely follows the text and illustrations in Ballard's* Finding the Titanic, *it complements this book well.*

Internet

Northern Nights Productions Titanic Division. (1997–1999). *The Titanic information site.* Retrieved September 3, 1999, from the World Wide Web: http://www.skarr.com/titanic.
> *This site contains general information on the* Titanic, *including a list of often asked questions.*

Hind, P. (1999). *The encyclopedia Titanica.* Retrieved September 3, 1999, from the World Wide Web: http://atschool.eduweb.co.uk/phind/home.html.
> *Besides general information on the* Titanic, *this site also has lists of passengers and crew, deck plans, photographs, movie shots of the* Titanic *in 1912 from archive films, and an animation showing the sinking of the* Titanic.

Geocities. (1999). *R.M.S. Titanic.* Retrieved September 3, 1999 from the World Wide Web: http://www.geocities.com/Rainforest/Vines/8059/titanic.htm.
> *This site includes a tour of the ship, a list of food and items carried on the ship, the cost of building the ship, and many facts about the mechanics of the* Titanic.

National Geographic. (1996). *I survived the Titanic.* Retrieved September 3, 1999, from the World Wide Web: http://www.nationalgeographic.com/media/world/9607/titanic.html.
> *This is an excerpt from an article in* National Geographic World, *July 1996, written by Jennifer Kirkpatrick, in which Ruth Becker, a 12-year-old survivor of the* Titanic, *tells her story.*

Discovery Online. (1996, 1997). *Titanic: Raising a legend.* Retrieved September 3, 1999, from the World Wide Web: http://www.discovery.com/area/science/titanic/titanicopener.html.
> *This is a report of the 1996 expedition to the* Titanic *that attempted to answer questions about the sinking of the ship and raised a piece of the ship's hull.*

National Maritime Museum. (1999). *Fact files: The Titanic.* Retrieved September 3, 1999, from the World Wide Web: http://www.nmm.ac.uk/ei/fact/index.htm.
> *This fact file for students and teachers about ships and ship building includes easy-to-read information in question and answer form.*

Global Online Adventure Learning Site. (1995–1999). *Sailing thru science: Understanding global navigation.* Retrieved September 3, 1999 from the World Wide Web: http://www.goals.com/sailscin/sailscin.htm.
> *The information on long-distance sailing and navigation includes an explanation of latitude, communication at sea, and the conversion of salt water into usable water.*

Other Works Cited

Commonwealth of Virginia Board of Education. (1995). *Standards of learning for Virginia public schools.* Richmond, VA: Author.

Fowler, D., & McCallum, S. (1998). *Expanding expectations language resource guide, Grades 4–6: Assessing.* Fairfax, VA: Fairfax County Public Schools.

TESOL. (1997). *ESL standards for pre-K–12 students.* Alexandria, VA: Author.

TESOL. (1998). *Managing the assessment process: A framework for measuring student attainment of the ESL standards* (TESOL Professional Paper No. 5). Alexandria, VA: Author.

TESOL. (in press). *Scenarios for ESL standards-based assessment.* Alexandria, VA: Author.

Touchstone Applied Science Associations. (1989). *Degrees of reading power.* Benbrook, TX: Author.

UNIT 3
Investigating How Much: Linear, Volume, and Mass Measurement

PAULA MERCHANT *and* LOUISE YOUNG

Introduction

The students are scattered across the tennis courts under a fall sun. Some pace while others crouch, moving a small object along one of the white lines. Every now and then there is a burst of laughter. Various students reach the end of a line and shout numbers to the others in their group. It is September, the leaves are turning, we are all new to each other, and the students are trying to figure out how to accurately measure the tennis court lines using seashells.

We initiated this unit as an icebreaker. There are so many introductions to be made at the beginning of the year that it is often very difficult for the teacher to try to sequence activities. Although this unit could be carried out at any time of the year, it works well at the beginning because it introduces each student to several crucial elements of our course at once. Students learn how to work in a group; complete a lab exercise and write a lab report; understand linear measurement, volume, and mass; and use the tools needed to perform these measurements. All this is accomplished before we hand out the first textbook.

Context

Grade level: Seventh grade

English proficiency levels: Mixed

Native languages of students: Multilingual low-incidence representation

Focus of instruction: Science and mathematics

Type of class: ESOL students in mainstream science class, with ESL academic support class

Length of unit: 3 weeks (20–30 hours)

Unit Overview

The unit is designed for a science class of heterogeneously grouped students. The ESOL students take the science class with native English speakers and receive additional support from the ESL teacher (Paula) during the science class and through a daily ESL academic support class. The science teacher (Louise) has also been trained in second language acquisition (SLA) and strategies for integrating language and content.

Our school is divided into teams. Ours is a seventh-grade heterogeneous group of approximately 100 students who are led by a team of teachers offering instruction in math, science, ESL, social studies, English, and special education.

Unit Overview: Linear, Volume, and Mass Measurement

Science Goals	ESL Standards	Assessment
Interact through words and actions while practicing each of the jobs on the lab team	Goal 2, Standard 1: Students will use English to interact in the classroom	Science content journal
		Anecdotal records
Work in groups to measure, problem solve, collect data, analyze data, and write conclusions	Goal 2, Standard 2: Students will use English to obtain, process, construct, and provide subject matter information in spoken and written form	Rubric correlated with state assessment for writing
		Three complete lab write-ups (line, volume, mass)
Use key measurement vocabulary with the proper tools and actions	Goal 2, Standard 3: Students will use appropriate learning strategies to construct and apply academic knowledge	Procedure for common activity
Identify many ways that measurement is integral to their lives		Secret line drawing
		Volume three-ways project
Demonstrate their understanding of linear measurement, volume, mass, and their differences	Goal 3, Standard 1: Students will use the appropriate language variety, register, and genre according to audience, purpose and setting	Instructions for using a triple beam balance
		Final project
		Students' input and interactions
	Goal 3, Standard 3: Students will use appropriate learning strategies to extend their communicative competence	Graphic organizers
		Student self-assessment

The unit overview shows the goals for the unit, the ESL standards addressed, and the activities used to assess achievement in science and ESL.

For the content in this unit, students learn how to use a ruler, graduated cylinder, and triple beam balance to perform the many measurements that are part of data analysis in their physics, chemistry, and biology work during the year.

The beauty of this unit, and of science in general, is that there is so much action, and there are so many manipulatives that the language of science can be learned in an experiential manner. The student banter that develops in a group approach allows ESOL students the opportunity to practice their English while the focus is on the task. Being a member of a working group invariably allows for good listening and discussion.

The erif is the unit of measurement used in this unit. It provides a touch of whimsy in what might otherwise be a very plodding progression. Our team is named the Firebirds. *Erif* is *fire* spelled backwards. Other teachers using this unit might not want to use the erif, but should try having the students measure with random objects before using the metric measurements—wonderful revelations result.

Because Paula is the only ESL teacher in her building, placing all 15 middle school ESOL students on the same team makes the task of providing an effective program easier. We can better meet the needs of ESOL learners because curriculum, instruction, and assessment become a collaborative effort among all content teachers. Common planning time, during which curriculum planning and communication about students are the primary goals, is built into our daily schedule. We use this team time to plan our instructional activities and assessment and to look at implications for English language learners. This time also gives us an opportunity to determine which coteaching models will best support English language learners for a particular class, unit, or activity.

Standards

When we met to think about the needs of English language learners and about how to plan this unit to help them meet our science goals and the ESL standards (TESOL, 1997), we thought about the following questions:

1. What are the implications of the science standards for an English language learner? How can the ESL standards serve as a bridge to the science activities, goals, and standards?

If all students are to reach high standards, teachers will have to begin looking at their curricula and instructional activities through many different lenses. As a content/ESL team, we analyze the science goals and plan instructional and assessment activities through an SLA lens. This is where the ESL standards can be aligned with and serve as a bridge to our science goals. We are able, unit by unit, to align the ESL standards and science goals, and to look at language and cultural implications in manageable parts, so language learning in the science classroom is maximized.

In analyzing the science goals and each activity, a team of teachers can brainstorm all of the possible implications and requirements for students to be able to perform tasks, including learning new vocabulary, concepts, and strategies. Before beginning the unit, we create a preliminary breakdown list and note strategies and progress indicators that we believe will show attainment of both the ESL standards and science goals. As we progress through the unit activities, we do a more in-depth daily analysis of the content and language, and plan the activities that will be addressed in the science classroom or in the ESL academic support class.

2. How can instructional activities in science be designed to individualize student learning and incorporate strategies that integrate both language and content?

One primary goal of standards-based reform efforts is to individualize instruction for all students. Science is a natural subject for facilitating language acquisition because the inquiry-based, collaborative approach encourages communication and provides many opportunities to see, hear, manipulate, speak about, and write about concepts. While students are working in groups, teachers can support learning through interaction and modeling, observing, and planning alternative or reinforcement activities. We also provide specific accommodations that will help students be successful using an inquiry approach, including modeling of collaborative work and direct instruction about expectations for appropriate group interaction. We also have many opportunities for assessment through the observation of students and documentation of performance. These inform our instruction and planning on a continuous basis.

One critical component of helping English language learners attain standards is to provide an environment where the students are engaged with rigorous content, where they know they can ask for clarification, and where concepts can be reinforced as necessary. A small-group setting, as in the ESL academic support class, allows the ESL teacher and students to assess together comprehension of material, and to prepare for the tasks that will be performed in science class. This support class gives a lot of individual attention to students, allows for one-on-one tutoring, and provides additional scaffolding, all based on the former schooling and proficiency levels of the students.

3. How will English language learners be assessed?

English language learners will be assessed in many different ways in the science and the ESL classrooms. Initial assessment of prior knowledge and proficiency guide the preliminary design of instruction. As the unit progresses, many forms of assessment are incorporated, including teacher observation, pen-and-pencil quizzes and tests, lab work, student self-assessment, group-work assessments, and content writing activities.

With a simple program on our computer system, progress indicators for each activity are transformed into a progress indicator checklist, as in the sample shown on pages 59–60, making classroom observation an easily documented task. We are thus prepared to recognize the many instances where a student may demonstrate achievement and comprehension. In addition, rubrics are introduced and become part of the routine of the year, making students active participants in their own assessment.

Scenarios for ESL Standards-Based Assessment (TESOL, in press) has been extremely helpful in providing concrete ideas for classroom assessment. *Managing the Assessment Process* (TESOL, 1998) has also provided a framework for assessment that benefits all students in a classroom. In particular it provides an outline of the stages of data collection and analysis, and has made us more aware of the many forms of assessment we use, and the many stakeholders who can participate in the assessment process.

4. What are the roles of the ESL and science teacher?

We are coaches, facilitators, interpreters, and evaluators, and we take on many other roles, even those of fictional characters. We are also learners, just as our students are. We each bring expertise from our fields, standards for our teaching, and the willingness to make a standards-based approach work, even if it takes several tries. We recognize that this is a process and that we need to evaluate the program, our lesson plans, and our priorities for managing our classroom time continuously. Our role on a team of teachers is to integrate curriculum and to ensure achievement for all students. This requires us to negotiate instructional decisions and to benefit from different perspectives,

Progress Indicator Checklist

Student Name:

Date	Observation/ Comments	Checklist for Progress Indicators
		Part 1: Introduce Lab Format and Jobs
		• follow directions to form groups
		• negotiate cooperative roles and task assignments
		• take turns when speaking in a group
		• sequence lab parts verbally and in writing
		• compare and contrast parts of lab verbally and in writing
		• use contextual clues
		Part 2: Use Linear Measurement
		• take turns when speaking in a group
		• share classroom materials and work successfully in a group
		• record observations
		• construct a chart synthesizing information
		• write a conclusion that addresses each of the questions
		• rephrase, explain, revise, and expand information
		• take notes to summarize the main points of brainstorming
		• observe language use and behaviors of peers
		• test appropriate use of newly acquired gestures and language
		Part 3: Measure Volume
		• join in a group response at the appropriate time
		• listen to and incorporate a peer's feedback regarding the lab
		• use polite forms to negotiate and reach consensus
		• take a position and support it orally or in writing
		• explain or demonstrate an estimation technique
		• write a procedure
		• verbalize relationships between new and previous information
		• take notes on a graphic organizer
		• use pictures to demonstrate comprehension

continued on page 60

Progress Indicator Checklist, *continued*

Date	Observation/ Comments	Checklist for Progress Indicators
		Part 4: Explore Mass
		• join in a group response at the appropriate time
		• listen to and incorporate a peer's feedback
		• use polite forms to negotiate and reach consensus
		• take a position and support it
		• compare and classify objects
		• gather and organize materials needed to complete a task
		• verbalize relationships between new and previously acquired information
		• create an instruction manual for the triple beam balance

---

with the goal of arriving at consensus. The input of a whole team of experts enriches this process and serves as a truly integrated professional development opportunity.

Activities, Part 1: Introduction to Writing and Performing Labs

In the introductory lessons, we introduce the strategies and assessment formats that will be used in science for the rest of the year. We are introducing the students to the measurement techniques that they will use in their science careers, and we are being introduced to the students as learners. We begin to establish the role of the ESL academic support classroom in their science studies.

Goal 2, Standard 1   To use English to achieve academically in all content areas: Students will use English to interact in the classroom.

Descriptors
- following oral and written directions
- participating in full-class, group, and pair discussions
- negotiating and managing interaction to accomplish tasks

Progress Indicators
- follow directions to form groups
- negotiate cooperative roles and task assignments
- take turns when speaking in a group

> **Goal 2, Standard 2** To use English to achieve academically in all content areas: Students will use English to obtain, process, construct, and provide subject matter information in spoken and written form.
>
> ### Descriptors
>
> - listening to, speaking, reading, and writing about subject matter information
> - analyzing, synthesizing, and inferring from information
> - understanding and producing technical vocabulary
>
> ### Progress Indicators
>
> - sequence lab parts verbally and in writing
> - compare and contrast parts of the lab verbally and in writing
> - use contextual clues

The team is broken up into classes of 22–26 students. We divide each class into lab groups of 4. Grouping is carefully planned yet flexible, sometimes allowing less proficient students to be seated together in a lab group, making accommodations and clarification of content manageable for both teachers. Other times, students are grouped with peers who speak the same native language so they can use their native languages as a tool for comprehension. Most often students are grouped with both native and nonnative English speakers in a lab group based on group dynamics. We switch lab groups throughout the year so students are exposed to a variety of personalities and learning styles. With clear roles within groups and frequent shifting of groups, students learn to be accountable for their own learning as well as the group task.

Student jobs (described below) are posted and rotated on a weekly basis:

Gatherer: Gets materials needed for activity

Cleaner: Puts away, cleans materials at the end of the activity

Work Monitor: Makes sure each person records necessary data, collects homework, hands out any paperwork

Schedule Monitor: Checks and signs assignment notebook, notes if a group member is absent and saves work for that individual, keeps track of time

The students pick up a syllabus (we call it the *Sci Fire News*) at the beginning of each week. It includes class activities and assignments for the entire week, plus any announcements. Students copy the homework assignments into their assignment notebooks so they are listed with all the other subjects. This routine allows the ESL teacher to answer clarification questions and to note any specific issues to address with students in the ESL academic support class. This syllabus keeps us all clear on expectations. The science teacher structures the week more fluidly, the ESL teacher can see what is going on in order to plan reinforcement and preclass activities, and the students can see what is expected of them.

In the science classroom, we relegate one large bulletin board to science vocabulary. This allows all students to refer to the board for spelling and ideas as they write about their work. It also provides an ongoing reference for English language learners in the class as they learn new content vocabulary and need visual access to key words they will be writing and speaking about in class. Students provide many creative ideas on how to display, categorize, and remember new terminology.

In the ESL classroom, we collect information on a daily basis through various assessment activities. In this first unit of the year, it is important to gather baseline information that will be noted and used as scaffolding for instruction and assessment for the unit. We use this information as we discuss student comprehension and progress and as we plan the accommodations we make each day. We also use this information at our daily team meeting to discuss student progress across content classes, and to validate instructional and assessment decisions.

To link ESL standards and science goals to daily class activities during a given day or period of time, we post laminated strips with the standards, descriptors, and progress indicators, written in understandable language, on the board. We end each class by relating the activities we did to these posted strips. Our goal in doing this is to make students more explicitly aware not only of expectations for class, but of the bigger picture of expectations in an age of standards, assessment, and accountability. By connecting class activities and student progress to these standards and progress indicators, students begin to assess their own learning and understand what is expected. Although some teachers caution against overemphasizing high-stakes assessment, we believe students become more confident when they are aware of what will be expected of them in such tests.

Corners Structure

The use of a corners structure in the ESL support class is one way to help meet the needs of a multilevel classroom. The teacher creates three stations, or corners, in the room, each focusing on an aspect of the activities that will follow in the science class, activities for which the students will most likely need additional reinforcement and preparation in terms of technical vocabulary. Below is an example showing how the corners methodology could be used with the first lesson, which is described in the next section.

PROCEDURE

- Each student is given a small blue notebook entitled *Science Content Journal*. This is a multipurpose journal that serves as an assessment tool as well as a personalized content dictionary and study guide.

- Students are assigned to groups. Each group is assigned to one of the three corners for 10 minutes and then instructed to proceed to the next corner.

- Students are given time to come together as a whole group to compile their findings and discuss difficulties and breakthroughs. In sharing their learning, students have an opportunity to use new vocabulary and the teacher can monitor both academic and social language development.

SAMPLE CORNER ACTIVITIES

Accessing and assessing prior knowledge: In their science content journals, students answer three questions written on a chart at the corner. Responses to the questions become a written sample that can be used to assess writing and extent of exposure to measurement in former schooling.

1. What is measurement?
2. What are some of the things in your life that you measure?
3. What are some of the words that you use when you measure or talk about measurement?

In addition, this activity gives students some advance time to think about the subject and to review or learn vocabulary necessary for science. The baseline information gleaned from this content writing sample is noted and shared with the science teacher. The illustration shows Laura's journal entry.

Laura's Journal Entry

Measurement is very inportant, measurement is a way of how to tell how long something is, or how short something is. You can also so measure the wigth of something is, the hight, or even the length. Measurement helps you in math, in work, in homework, and many more.

Measurement Can help many people. It can help you when your or someone khow makes houses, like an artiquet. It can also help in Math home work, or even in science, like what were doing. Were doing an experiment called 48 apples wich in it you measure apples.

Measure-ment is inportant in many different ways. Firts; it helps you, Second; i fun to learn, and Third; it is important, and thats not all.

They are some words that realate to measurent for example; math or measureing.

Building vocabulary: Students focus on the language of measurement as they encounter related vocabulary in children's literature, Web sites, recipes, poems, and other written materials. Students are given a model chart to copy into their science content journals and asked to find as many measurement words as they can in the materials. They record the words on the chart. For homework, students will finish the chart by using their bilingual dictionaries to clarify any new words they have encountered. Students have opportunities to use these materials over the course of the week and to create their own measurement dictionaries, which they use to contribute to the measurement vocabulary board in the science classroom.

Word Splash Original

First   **Finally**

Next

Third

In conclusion

After that

Second   **To sum up**

Before

Following....

Word splash and sentence strips: As a group the students put the sequence words on the **word splash** page in order (see p. 64). After reviewing sequence terms, each person chooses one of the **sentence strips** from the packet. As a group they interact to sequence the sentence strips correctly. Then they add the sequence words from the word splash cards. The result is a properly sequenced procedure. Students then discuss the importance of the words that are used to make the sequence clear. One student's completed paper with the word splash and sentence strips is shown.

Word Splash and Sentence Strips

WORD SPLASH

Following.... Pick a corner you a.

First You start make shure thats the corner you want to measure first.

Second Put the ruler next to your corner.

Third make shure that the ruler is on the centimeter side.

Next Measure it and write it down on a peice of paper

Finally do the same on

Introduction of Lab Format and Jobs

Procedure

- Prior to beginning each unit, Paula provides a student overview of the unit (see p. 67) and explicitly discusses what will be expected in terms of performance in science class. She spends extra time reinforcing new concepts through a variety of activities and allows additional time for minilessons throughout the writing process.

- To provide an ongoing assessment of writing, Paula introduces students to the writing rubric that she and Louise use to assess students' writing in their science and ESL/language arts classes. She gives them a writing checklist based on the rubric, to be used for self-assessment and guidance as they write. The academic support class allows additional time to meet one-on-one with students, using the criteria given on the rubric to help them see how they can improve and how they can be partners in their own assessment and the assessment of their peers. The writing rubric directly reflects the criteria on the state performance assessment for writing, which the students take in the eighth grade, and it also incorporates a section on language production based in an SLA context. Students become experts and, by the middle of the year, are able to be good negotiators in peer review activities and in determining their grades. Weaving assessment and instruction through activities and making expectations for meeting standards explicit for students are critical components of standards-based instruction. The promise we see in this approach becomes a reality when teachers and their students are able to develop this agreement on performance.

- In the science class, Louise introduces students to the lab report format (title, purpose, materials, procedure, results, conclusion). To model the format of the procedure section, Louise gives students a series of scrambled directions for doing a small task and asks them to put the directions in order. Then she hands out the first lab assignment, which is shown on page 68, on measuring length. Students copy the lab report in the correct order and add labeled data charts ready to receive data. Then each student is assigned a lab group role for the week.

- Homework: Students write a procedure for how to do something quite basic, such as putting on a sweater, making a sandwich, or pouring a glass of milk. Louise reminds them to make it very detailed. The next day, Louise plays a character who is very literal and tries to follow several of the lab procedures, always misinterpreting their directions. It is an enjoyable reminder about being explicit and accurate when writing a procedure.

Assessment and Support

Paula monitors students informally as they begin writing their procedures, to see if more support is needed with this kind of precise writing. Some students may consult their science content journals to use the sequencing strips as a reference. This is an example of the scaffolding that is created between the two classroom settings, which helps students participate more fully. Students are told to bring their draft procedures to the ESL academic support class the next day for editing and rewriting. Paula meets with students one-on-one to talk about their written work. She uses this conference to determine a student's writing needs, which become the basis for minilessons. In this confer-

Student Overview

The Erif: A Story about
Linear, Volume and Mass Measurement

The Keeper helps you to be a responsible lab group member, solve problems
and ask good questions about Science using a very special
Firebird <u>unit of measurement</u> called the erif!

The Keeper's Visits:

Linear Measurement
Creative measurement techniques
New words
Tools

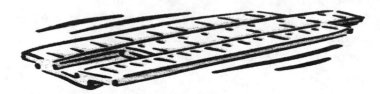

Measurement of Volume
Irregular Objects
Cubes and Blocks
Liquids
New words
Tools

Measurement of Mass
Mass vs. Weight
Goldilocks and the 3 Bears
New words
Tools

3-in-1 Tool Expo
Firebird Inventors, show us what you've got!

First Lab Assignment

Lab 1: Line Lab—Measuring Length

Purpose or problem: To find out the length of each of five small objects and each line on half of a tennis court

Materials:

five small objects	measuring device 1
tennis court with lines	measuring device 2
clipboard when going to tennis court	

Procedure:

First measuring day:
1. Receive and record the first measuring device.
2. Select and measure five of the small objects on display.
3. Record your measurements on a chart under Results.

Second measuring day:
1. Using the same measuring device from day one, measure all the lines on one side of the tennis court.
2. Record your measurements on a chart under Results.

Third measuring day:
1. Convert your measurements of the small objects and the tennis court lines into the unit on measuring device 2.
2. Add your conversions to the chart so that you now have all measurements on one chart.

Results: *(Place empty chart here with columns labeled.)*

Conclusion: *(Answer the following questions in complete sentences.)*
- What problems did you have with the erif?
- What problems did you have with the centimeter?
- Which do you prefer using and why?
- Are your measuring needs different when the object is small or large?

ence, she is able to learn through written and spoken modes what science content the student has understood.

Activities, Part 2: Measuring Small Objects With the Erif

This section on linear measurement leads students from a fictional system of measurement to a real system in order to increase their understanding of the meaning of linear measurement. The voice below is that of a fictional character called the *Keeper* (played by Louise, the science teacher), who introduces each measurement unit and leads students through stages of their inquiry:

In Firebird country, we have been measuring for centuries using tiny shells. Each shell is called an erif. I am the Keeper of the Erif. I hold the erifs and dispense them when necessary. Your job is to measure the length of five of the small objects in the collection to the nearest erif. I am very nervous about losing my erifs and will only let you have yours for 1 minute. You will have to find a way to record the erif before giving it back to me.

We use a collection of small objects, blocks, square plastic containers or milk cartons with the tops cut off, paper cups, large linear areas to measure, and meter sticks or tapes for these activities.

Goal 2, Standard 1 To use English to achieve academically in all content areas: Students will use English to interact in the classroom.

Descriptors

- following oral and written directions, implicit and explicit
- requesting and providing clarification
- negotiating and managing interaction to accomplish tasks

Progress Indicators

- take turns when speaking in a group
- share classroom materials and work successfully with a group

---

Goal 2, Standard 2 To use English to achieve academically in all content areas: Students will use English to obtain, process, construct, and provide subject matter information in spoken and written form.

Descriptors

- demonstrating knowledge through application in a variety of contexts
- analyzing, synthesizing, and inferring from information
- selecting, connecting, and explaining information

Progress Indicators

- record observations
- construct a chart synthesizing information
- write a conclusion that addresses each of the questions clearly

Goal 2, Standard 3   To use English to achieve academically in all content areas: Students will use appropriate learning strategies to construct and apply academic knowledge.

Descriptors

- actively connecting new information to information previously learned
- evaluating one's own success in a completed learning task

Progress Indicators

- rephrase, explain, revise, and expand oral or written information to check comprehension
- take notes to summarize the main points of brainstorming

Goal 3, Standard 3   To use English in socially and culturally appropriate ways: Students will use appropriate learning strategies to extend their communicative competence.

Descriptor

- observing and modeling how others speak and behave in a particular situation or setting

Progress Indicators

- observe language use and behaviors of peers in different settings
- test appropriate use of newly acquired gestures and language

Measure Small Objects

PROCEDURE

- The Keeper gives each group their erif for 1 minute. She then collects the erifs.
- Students measure their objects and record the data in the results section of the lab report (the title, purpose, materials, and procedure were copied the day before). As the students work in their groups, teachers circulate and facilitate as necessary.
- Homework: Students create a line drawing and measure each line in erifs. They record the measurements on the lines and reveal their design to

Using prepositions and directional words to talk about location is often difficult for students with very limited English proficiency. The use of a graphic organizer depicting these words visually helps these students participate more easily in this activity. When necessary, the ESL teacher can also teach a minilesson in advance, giving students who need it an introduction to the use of the imperative and the terminology needed to participate.

no one. ESOL students are provided with a graphic organizer of directional terminology in order to help them describe their line drawings the next day.

Measure the Tennis Court

PROCEDURE

- Warm-up: Holding their homework designs, the students sit back to back. They take turns describing their designs to their partners, erifs and all, and the partners draw what they hear.
- Paula and Louise take the students to a larger area to measure longer linear measurements: windows, desks, bricks, lines in a parking lot, fences—anything will do. We use the lines on the tennis court. The groups are given very little time to measure the prescribed lengths, necessitating a group strategy. They record these new, longer measurements on charts of their own making.

Conversion

PROCEDURE

- The Keeper reappears, saying: "No more erifs will be used to measure lines. You must show all of your measurements with this new unit, called the centimeter, which is marked on this stick, called a ruler. I will allow you to have your erif back for just a minute and then will give you your new tool, a centimeter ruler. You must convert all your measurements to centimeters. Do so on your chart."
- Paula and Louise help students as they work in groups to convert their measurements of the small objects and the tennis court lines into the units on their centimeter rulers and record their conversions. Additional time is provided in the ESL class to model conversions, and to make sure that students understand that *convert* means to change.
- In preparation for writing conclusions, Paula introduces the **big ideas/small details T-graph,** which will be used in the ESL classes as an organizer for all writing that is expository in nature. Using this organizer helps students distinguish between main ideas and details and master the structure of a paragraph. Eventually, students are able to extend the use of this organizer to planning a five-paragraph essay.

For students who need more help distinguishing between main ideas and details, or for students with limited formal schooling who may not be writing full sentences, index cards containing words that show topics and subtopics, big ideas and little details can be used. Students can read these words and place them in an order that shows an understanding of the structure of a good paragraph, with a main idea and supporting details. A more kinesthetic approach might involve students reading their cards, discussing the relationship among all of the cards, putting the parts together in a whole, and creating a human structure that represents the structure of the paragraph.

Conclusion Writing

PROCEDURE

- The students' first attempt at writing a conclusion is very structured. They are asked to answer the following questions in complete sentences:

  What problems did you have with the erif?

  What problems did you have with the centimeter?

  Which do you prefer using and why?

  Are your measuring needs different when the object is small or large?

ASSESSMENT

Copies of the self-assessment and group assessment sheets that we use are shown on pages 72–73. We ask

K-W-L-H charts are another way to document newly acquired knowledge, assess student learning, facilitate conclusion development, and help students monitor their own learning. The addition of the H was suggested by a colleague, who asks students, as they discuss their K-W-L charts, "How did you get the information or answer in the K column?" This addition explicitly validates the use of many of the strategies introduced to the students in a unit. K-W-L-H charting is one of the strategies that benefits all students, but particularly those learning English. It is a self-assessment where students articulate their own learning strategies and metacognition.

Self-Assessment Sheet

Name:_____

Date:_____

What I learned today in science:

_____

_____

Please rate yourself in your group work in science today.

   1 = Rarely   3 = Sometimes   5 = Often

1. I understood the task.	1	3	5
2. I listened to and understood group members.	1	3	5
3. I asked questions.	1	3	5
4. I gave my opinion and ideas to the group.	1	3	5

What was easy about science today?

What was difficult?

Do you think your group worked well together? Why or why not?

What questions do you have about class today?

I need extra help.   _____Yes   _____No

```
Group Assessment Sheet

Date:_____

Activity: _____

_____

Names and Roles of Group Members

Name                          Role
1.
2.
3.
4.


Did your group accomplish the task? What was easy? What was difficult?

What was easy about working as a group? What was difficult?

Rate your working as a group
    (1 = Excellent          3 = So-so          5 = Needs Improvement)
1.  We accomplished our task.                            1    3    5
    Comments:

2.  Every group member participated.                     1    3    5
    Comments:

3.  Group members listened to each other.                1    3    5
    Comments:

4.  Group members made decisions together.               1    3    5
    Comments:

5.  Group members encouraged each other to share ideas.  1    3    5
    Comments:
```

students to fill them out at the conclusion of this first lab, so each of them will think about the group as a whole and their role in the group.

Activities, Part 3: The Keeper Introduces Volume

This section builds on the introduction to how to participate in and write up a lab. At the same time we introduce a new type of measurement, which necessitates making choices in tools and methods. The Keeper has to provide more direct instruction and modeling for this type of measurement.

Before we begin, we collect small objects, blocks, small plastic containers, cartons with tops cut off, graduated cylinders, overflow cups, rulers or tapes, paper, small cups of sand, and the erifs.

Goal 2, Standard 1 To use English to achieve academically in all content areas: Students will use English to interact in the classroom.

Descriptors

- requesting and providing clarification
- participating in full-class, group, and pair discussions

Progress Indicators

- join in a group response at the appropriate time
- listen to and incorporate a peer's feedback regarding the lab
- use polite forms to negotiate and reach consensus

Goal 2, Standard 2 To use English to achieve academically in all content areas: Students will use English to obtain, process, construct, and provide subject matter information in spoken and written form.

Descriptors

- hypothesizing and predicting
- selecting, connecting, and explaining information
- demonstrating knowledge through application in a variety of contexts

Progress Indicators

- take a position and support it orally or in writing
- explain or demonstrate an estimation technique
- write a procedure

continued on page 75

Pre-Lab 2: Volume

PROCEDURE

- The Keeper leads a discussion on how to figure out how many erifs fill up the space of various objects, or volume: "Your next job is to find out how many erifs would fill up the space in each of your five small objects. How could you do this?"

- The Keeper records student suggestions. They might include holding erifs up against the objects, making more erifs out of tissue or paper towels, or borrowing erifs. "I do not want you to attempt your measurements today. Today you must write a title, purpose, materials, and procedure for how you intend to measure volume in erifs. You will do the measurements tomorrow."

- We encourage students to try unique approaches to solving this problem.

Goal 2, Standard 3 To use English to achieve academically in all content areas: Students will use appropriate learning strategies to construct and apply academic knowledge.

Descriptors

- actively connecting new information to information previously learned
- planning how and when to use cognitive strategies and applying them appropriately to a learning task
- taking notes to record important information and aid one's own learning

Progress Indicators

- verbalize and write relationships between new information and information previously learned in another setting
- take notes on a graphic organizer
- use pictures to demonstrate comprehension of the processes of measuring volume

---

- Homework: Students draw a picture and describe the difference between measuring lines and measuring volume using new and old words from their science content journals.

ASSESSMENT AND SUPPORT

In the ESL academic support class, Paula collects the lab write-ups to determine students' understanding. As a class, the group works together to brainstorm ways to solve the problem of measuring volume. As the students express themselves, they add new measurement vocabulary *(width, cube, depth, height)* to their science content journals. Paula also uses the lab assessment shown on page 76 as a guiding tool to give students specific feedback about their lab write-ups.

Estimating the Volume of Small Objects

PROCEDURE

- The Keeper returns and speaks: "You must measure five objects using your own special techniques to find out how many erifs of space fill up each of your objects. I will return at the end of class."
- In their lab groups, students try out the techniques they developed by measuring the volume of five small objects using erifs.
- At the conclusion of class the Keeper shows up again: "I have been put in charge of a new measurement unit for volume. It is called the cubic centimeter. We will make a cubic centimeter now so that you can see how much volume it is. Please make a little box of paper that is one centimeter on each edge."
- Each student is given paper and a ruler and asked to construct a cubic centimeter.

Sample Lab Assessment

Name _____

Presentation
- all six lab parts spelled properly (1)_____
- all six lab parts included (1)_____
- neat writing and ruler lines (1)_____

Content
- title, purpose, materials complete (1)_____
- procedure clear and complete (numbered steps) (1)_____
- results (data) complete (1)_____

Conclusion
- full sentences/complete thoughts (2)_____
- concise (2)_____
- thorough (2)_____

- Homework: Students write a procedure for how to make a cubic centimeter out of paper.

Cubic Centimeter and Milliliter

PROCEDURE

- The Keeper makes the connection that 1 cubic centimeter is the same amount of space as 1 milliliter by having students fill the cubic centimeter that they made with sand, and then pour the sand into a graduated cylinder. She tells students: "Now we will learn how to use the cubic centimeter or milliliter to measure the volume of your five objects. There are several techniques and tools that you can choose. Please pay close attention!"

- The Keeper presents three ways to measure volume, modeling each as she explains it to the students.

- Paula gives the students a worksheet to fill out as they listen to the Keeper describe the different ways of measuring volume and the tools necessary to do so. A word bank is provided at the bottom of the page. One student's completed worksheet is shown on page 77.

- Later, in the ESL academic support class with Paula, students work briefly together to measure volume three different ways and to verbalize these procedures.

ASSESSMENT AND HOMEWORK

Each student creates an instruction manual for next year's students on the three ways to determine the volume of an object. Illustrations, words, computer graphics, or video productions are all possibilities. Through this activity students are able to demonstrate their understanding of volume measurement, new tools, and the use of new content vocabulary.

Completed Worksheet

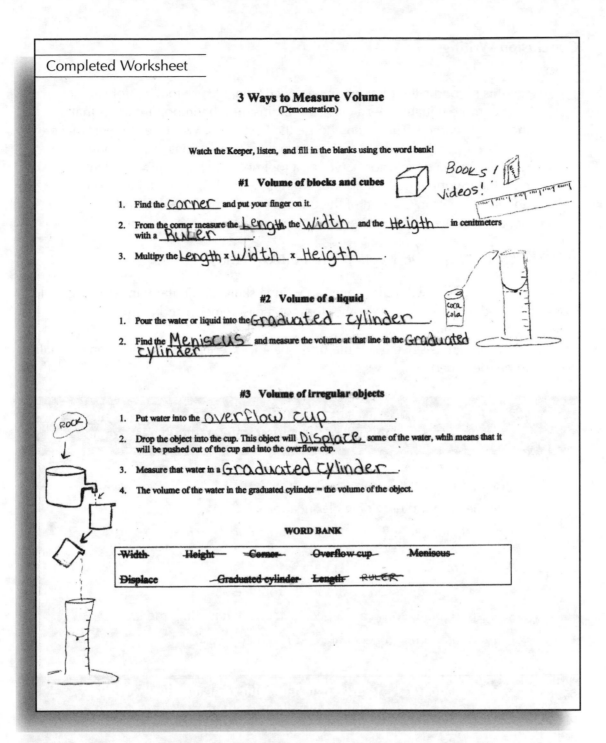

3 Ways to Measure Volume
(Demonstration)

Watch the Keeper, listen, and fill in the blanks using the word bank!

#1 Volume of blocks and cubes

1. Find the ___corner___ and put your finger on it.

2. From the corner measure the ___Length___, the ___Width___ and the ___Heigth___ in cenitmeters with a ___Ruler___.

3. Multipy the ___Length___ x ___Width___ x ___Heigth___.

BOOKS! Videos!

#2 Volume of a liquid

1. Pour the water or liquid into the ___Graduated cylinder___.

2. Find the ___Meniscus___ and measure the volume at that line in the ___Graduated cylinder___.

#3 Volume of irregular objects

ROCK

1. Put water into the ___overflow cup___.

2. Drop the object into the cup. This object will ___Disolace___ some of the water, whih means that it will be pushed out of the cup and into the overflow cup.

3. Measure that water in a ___Graduated cylinder___.

4. The volume of the water in the graduated cylinder = the volume of the object.

WORD BANK

~~Width~~	~~Height~~	~~Corner~~	~~Overflow cup~~	~~Meniscus~~
~~Displace~~		~~Graduated cylinder~~	~~Length~~	~~RULER~~

Measuring Volume

PROCEDURE

- The Keeper returns: "Today you will use the appropriate method to measure your five objects in centimeters or milliliters. Please measure each object twice because I need complete accuracy."

- Students gather rulers, overflow cups, graduated cylinders, and water, as well as their five objects. Each group has to agree on the appropriate method to determine the volume of each of the objects. After measuring, all numbers are recorded in data charts.

- Homework: Students continue with the project from the night before.

Conclusion Writing

PROCEDURE

- On this second attempt at writing a conclusion, we are looking for students to take more initiative. As a class, we brainstorm the important ideas that they have learned. They then choose the best ideas. We have students make a big ideas/small details T-graph to plan their conclusions. The graphic planner for the conclusion serves as a tool not only for helping students plan their writing, but also for determining what they have understood about concepts in this part of the unit. They will then use this graphic organizer to help them write good paragraphs for their conclusions.

Activities, Part 4: The Keeper Introduces Mass

In this section, students will refine their lab writing skills, particularly in writing conclusions; be introduced to mass as another form of measurement; and connect all three types of measurement in a final project.

For measuring mass, we use triple beam balances, erifs, and a collection of small objects to be measured.

Goal 2, Standard 1 **To use English to achieve academically in all content areas: Students will use English to interact in the classroom.**

Descriptors

- requesting and providing clarification
- participating in full-class, group, and pair discussions

Progress Indicators

- join in a group response at the appropriate time
- listen to and incorporate a peer's feedback regarding the lab
- use polite forms to negotiate and reach consensus

Goal 2, Standard 2 **To use English to achieve academically in all content areas: Students will use English to obtain, process, construct, and provide subject matter information in spoken and written form.**

Descriptors

- hypothesizing and predicting
- selecting, connecting, and explaining information
- responding to the work of peers and others

Progress Indicators

- take a position and support it orally or in writing
- compare and classify objects
- gather and organize the appropriate materials needed to complete a task

Goal 2, Standard 3 To use English to achieve academically in all content areas: Students will use appropriate learning strategies to construct and apply academic knowledge.

Descriptors

- actively connecting new information to information previously learned
- planning how and when to use cognitive strategies and applying them appropriately to a learning task

Progress Indicators

- verbalize and write relationships between new information and information previously learned in another setting

Goal 3, Standard 1 To use English in socially and culturally appropriate ways: Students will use the appropriate language variety, register, and genre according to audience, purpose, and setting.

Descriptor

- using a variety of writing styles appropriate for different audiences, purposes, and settings

Progress Indicator

- create an instruction manual for the Triple Beam Balance Company

Pre-Lab 3: Mass and Weight

PROCEDURE

- The Keeper presents the essence of mass:

  Mass is how much matter exists in an object. I can hold a rock in one hand and a pencil in the other hand, and even if their volume is the same, the rock will have more mass. I need you to work with erifs again but this time to measure the mass of your five small objects. How can you compare the mass of an erif with the mass of another object? You must figure out if your object is *less than, equal to,* or *more than* an erif. How can you do that?

- The Keeper records suggestions from the students, which may include using levers or hefting the objects.
- Students then prepare the third lab by writing the title, purpose, materials, and procedure, and making a data chart.
- Homework: Students finish the lab preparation. Each student should design a system to measure mass in erifs or sketch out a variety of ways it could be done.

Comparing Mass

PROCEDURE

- The Keeper returns to watch the students attempt to measure mass in erifs: "Today you must use your plan to measure the mass of each of your five objects in erifs. I will ask that each measurement be done at least twice for accuracy."

- Working in their lab groups, students try out the techniques they designed for measuring mass using erifs.

- In order to review what was learned in class and to prepare for the Keeper's visit the next day, Paula uses the ESL support class to design a graphic representation of the Keeper's visits to the science class. Students note the sequence of her visits, the purpose of each visit, and the main ideas they have learned from her visits. As a class these main ideas are discussed and predictions are made about her visit the next day. This clarification and review assists the students as they think about their writing assignment for science class that night.

ASSESSMENT AND HOMEWORK

Students predict what is going to happen when the Keeper comes tomorrow. What will she say? What kind of tool will she bring? This is an enjoyable opportunity for students to demonstrate what the Keeper will do based on her previous visits and the routine she has used. It also provides an opportunity to articulate the essence of each type of measurement and the tools that make it easier.

Triple Beam Balance

- The Keeper arrives to present the new measurement, called the gram. She also introduces the triple beam balance as the tool that will find the mass of items in grams: "Today we will use a new measurement for mass. It is called the gram. This is the tool that will allow you to find mass. It is called a triple beam balance. Please examine your new tool."

- Each group gets a balance. They adjust it and practice finding the mass of items of their own choice.

Although digital balances are what we use later in the year, the triple beam balance is an excellent way to review place value. We instruct the students to try the masses in order from heaviest to lightest. The story of Goldilocks and the three bears is a wonderful way to illustrate this technique: Goldilocks always tried the Papa Bear item first. Modeling the sliding of the masses to achieve balance on the tool helps all students, but is crucial for those who have low proficiency in English because it provides visual cues and an opportunity for imitation.

ASSESSMENT AND HOMEWORK

Students pretend they work for the Triple Beam Balance Company. Their job is to write the instruction sheet to be included in the package with the triple beam balance. ESOL students are encouraged to use their native languages. We make sure we allow plenty of time to explain the homework so students can sketch the triple beam to include in their homework instruction sheets if they desire.

Finding Mass

PROCEDURE

- The Keeper tries several of the homework instructions as a volunteer student reads them. She also explains how to estimate when the balance indicates a space between lines.

- The Keeper says: "Each group must now use the triple beam balance to find the mass of five objects to the nearest tenth of a gram. Be sure everyone gets a chance to try this, and remember to work from the largest mass on the balance to the smallest!"

- Each student measures five objects to the nearest tenth of a gram and records these measurements on the data chart for this lab.

- Homework: Students write up the questions they would like to answer in the conclusion.

Writing a Conclusion

PROCEDURE

- After a quick group sharing and discussion of the questions each student has chosen, each writes a conclusion in full sentences and in paragraphs (without the question/answer mode used in the beginning). Students are encouraged to use the big ideas/small details strategy that they have been practicing.

ASSESSMENT

As students write this third lab report, the teachers can observe and record their use of the strategies that have been introduced over the course of the three measurement sections. Students are now used to writing lab reports, especially the specific types of writing required for procedures and conclusions.

Final Projects/Assessments

PROCEDURE

- Louise gives students a paper-and-pencil quiz accompanied by graphics to test their understanding of the major ideas related to measurement. The following day, she introduces ideas for a culminating project. Students choose one of the project ideas.

- These ideas reflect the kinds of open-ended assessment problems that students need to solve on the Grade 8 state science assessment. The project is entered into the student science and ESL portfolio with teacher, peer, and self-assessment rubrics; photographs; and a paragraph where students are asked to describe how their project demonstrates their learning in this unit. Each project requires students to incorporate science concepts from each measurement section and new science terminology. A sample grading rubric for the tool inventions is shown on page 82.

- Louise uses the science lab notebook, which will hold each of the three lab reports and the final project, as an assessment of how the students apply new knowledge and use new language.

Grading Rubric

Three-in-One Tool

Name of Inventor_____

Please use this checklist to guide your work. This checklist will be collected with your tool.

_____ My project has three tools for measuring lines, volume, and mass. (6 points)

_____ Each has invented units. (4 points)

_____ Units are clearly marked. (2 points)

_____ My tool has a package. (2 points)

_____ My name and the name of my tool are on the package. (2 points)

_____ I have written instructions for using my tool. (2 points)

_____ My instructions are clear and complete. (2 points)

Sample Projects

- Tool inventions: Students create a three-in-one tool that uses invented units of measurement. The tool can measure length, volume, and mass. Along with design, each tool needs to come with its own instructions for use and packaging. We have a "Tool Expo" where the students have an opportunity to move from tool to tool, trying them out. Students use a rating sheet for each tool in the expo. They write up a review of their favorites for the team newspaper.

- Challenges: Students create a raft that will hold a volume of sand afloat for 2 minutes. Students must give the dimensions of the raft, including its length, width, mass, and the volume of sand it must hold.

- Experiment: Groups of students design an experiment to determine the answer to a question such as: Do large volume acorns have a larger mass than small volume acorns? How would you find the volume of a human?

Additional Information

The middle school philosophy, which promotes teams and interdisciplinary curriculum mapping, is a wonderful structure in which to work and one that naturally lends itself to the bridging of ESL standards with content standards. For teachers to truly coteach and to share in the process of curriculum development and assessment, schools must provide time for teachers to reflect on their practice, to share strategies, and to meet to develop curriculum units that will address English language learners but that ultimately benefit all students.

In low-incidence ESL programs, we may find ourselves in situations where students do not have adequate services to ensure an equal educational opportunity. Resources are often scarce, and teachers and administrators may have no formal training in SLA, or in programming structures and policies that support bilingual/bicultural students. The ESL standards can be used for advocacy purposes within a district, building, or classroom in several ways:

- The ESL standards are featured in the quality indicators used by the six national school accreditation boards ("New K–12 Accreditation Process," 1998). By sharing this information with the principals and superintendent, we were able to bring some initial attention to the ESL standards, which have not been officially adopted in our state, but which will inevitably be a part of the process of school accreditation. As a result, we were able to form a district team focusing on English language learners, to create an action plan, and to apply for a professional development grant supporting its implementation. The result has been a program to train teachers that will spread throughout the district.

- The "Access Brochure" (Appendix A in *ESL Standards for Pre-K–12 Students*, TESOL, 1997) can also be used by a district team, teacher, or school site council interested in assessing the response of a school or district to English language learners. It is a useful tool in looking at student access to rigorous curricula, equitable assessment, a positive learning environment, and full delivery of services. In response to results of this self-assessment as a school and district, our middle school site council has been able to incorporate specific goals into the school improvement plan, thereby improving the education of English language learners in our school.

- The introduction to *ESL Standards for Pre-K–12 Students* (TESOL, 1997) incorporates a rationale for ESL standards, key statements about SLA, and myths surrounding SLA. This part of the document can easily be used to plan individual teacher responses to misconceptions and to plan professional development modules within a team meeting or within a school.

- However the ESL standards are incorporated into our programs, the spirit of standards-based reform efforts needs to be the context in which we communicate to, about, and on behalf of our English language learners.

REFERENCES AND RESOURCES

Science Series

Aldrige, B., Aiuto, R., Ballinger, J., Barefoot, A., Crow, L., Feather, R. M., Jr., Kaskel, A., Kramer, C., Ortleb, E., Snyder, S., & Zitzewitz, P. W. (1995). *Science interactions.* Westerville, OH: Glencoe/McGraw-Hill.

Maton, A., Hopkins, J., Johnson, S., LaHart, D., McLaughlin, C. W., Warner, M. Q., & Wright, J. D. (1994). *Prentice Hall science: The nature of science.* Englewood Cliffs, NJ: Prentice Hall.

Morrison, E. S., Moore, A., Armour, N., Hammond, A., Haysom, J., Nicoll, E., & Smyth, M. (1997). *SciencePlus.* Austin, TX: Holt, Rinehart & Winston.

Works Cited

New K–12 accreditation process features TESOL standards. (1998, February/March). *TESOL Matters, 8*(1), 5.

TESOL. (1997). *ESL standards for pre-K–12 students.* Alexandria, VA: Author.

TESOL. (1998). *Managing the assessment process: A framework for measuring student attainment of the ESL standards* (TESOL Professional Paper No. 5). Alexandria, VA: Author.

TESOL. (in press). *Scenarios for ESL standards-based assessment.* Alexandria, VA: Author.

UNIT 4
Mastering the Art of Persuasion: Marketing and the Media

SUSAN SILLIVAN

Introduction

Room 102 is in seeming disarray. Desks and chairs have been pushed to the back of the room. Small groups of students are scattered throughout the room, all busily and noisily engaged. In one corner, a girl is singing a jingle, trying to coordinate movements with her words. Two boys are practicing the rhythmic sounds of a rap song, crossing out words and adding others as they consider their work. One stands and recites a line, emphasizing his beat with pumping arms and an abrupt leg split. The voice of another student, extolling the virtues of a limitless credit card, rises and falls as he tries out different tones and intonations.

In front of the class, a large open area serves as a stage. There, two students stand before floral patterned material that has been carefully tacked up to conceal the blackboard. Three other students stand some distance away, two holding large pieces of poster paper that serve as cue cards. The third operates a video camera. "Yo! Quiet!" booms Ramón, the apparent director, and the room's decibel level falls. The two boys begin to deliver their lines, but a problem quickly develops:

Ramón: Action!
Ajit: Welcome to the J and A Café!

Context

Grade level: Eighth grade

English proficiency levels: Intermediate, advanced

Native languages of students: Mixed; predominantly Spanish, Chinese, Punjabi

Focus of instruction: ESL/language arts

Type of class: ESL class, one period per day plus one double period per cycle

Length of unit: 4–5 weeks

> Juan: Hi, friends! Have you tried our new Sandwich Spectacular?
>
> Ajit: It's the greatest—four layers of delicious stuff.
>
> Ramón: Cut! You can't say stuff. How will the people know what stuff is?
>
> Juan: Yeah, stuff could be anything. Look at your cue card . . . .
>
> With the "Cut!" order, voice levels and activity return to normal. Ajit and Juan go off in search of the thesaurus.

All of these students are in the process of producing their own television commercials. They have created advertisements for their own restaurant, product, or service as part of an ongoing unit on persuasive writing, and are preparing for the final step of the activity, filming the performance.

Unit Overview

This unit on the theme of mastering the art of persuasion is designed to be the culminating unit in a yearlong ESL/language arts course. I chose the medium of advertising as a familiar way in which to present the concept of persuasion. Although students had some limited experience working on standards-based lessons, this was the first to incorporate fully both the ESL standards and the performance standards developed by the National Center on Education and the Economy (1998), commonly referred to as New Standards. The New Standards set performance standards in the areas of English language arts, mathematics, science, and applied learning. Student progress and level of achievement are determined by the administration of a standards-based examination, portfolios, and teacher observation. Students are categorized as having exceeded standards, having met standards, or not yet having met standards. Those who have yet to meet the standards may receive remediation.

The unit is based on a New Standards requirement that students produce a persuasive essay. Designed to occupy a 4- to 5-week time frame, it requires that students work in class and at home. During this period, all homework assignments relate directly to the class activities. After-school tutoring sessions are available 4 days a week for those students who need or wish to receive extra help.

My students perform best when they begin with receptive language skills. All four language skills are present in almost every lesson, but I try to design the overall unit so it builds from the most comfortable skill, listening, to that which requires the most demanding individual production of language, writing. It should be noted that although academic reading can be quite difficult for second language students, supporting their efforts through scaffolding can help them be successful. I do this in several ways: The reading I begin with is in a simple form; it is always read aloud in class. Introductory activities relate the reading to students' own experiences, which helps them comprehend better.

My goals for the unit are that students will

- use print and electronic media to gather information

- evaluate print and electronic advertising

- broaden their vocabulary base through the use of the thesaurus

- demonstrate a general understanding of advertising through the creation of various advertisements, both oral and written

- apply previously learned grammar and writing skills (e.g., comparison of adjectives, paragraph construction, variety in sentence types) in these advertisements
- use process writing to produce a persuasive essay in the form of an editorial

The unit overview shows the structure of the unit.

Standards

Implementing *ESL Standards for Pre-K–12 Students* (TESOL, 1997) in my class has changed my approach to unit planning. I now consider the goals and standards in my

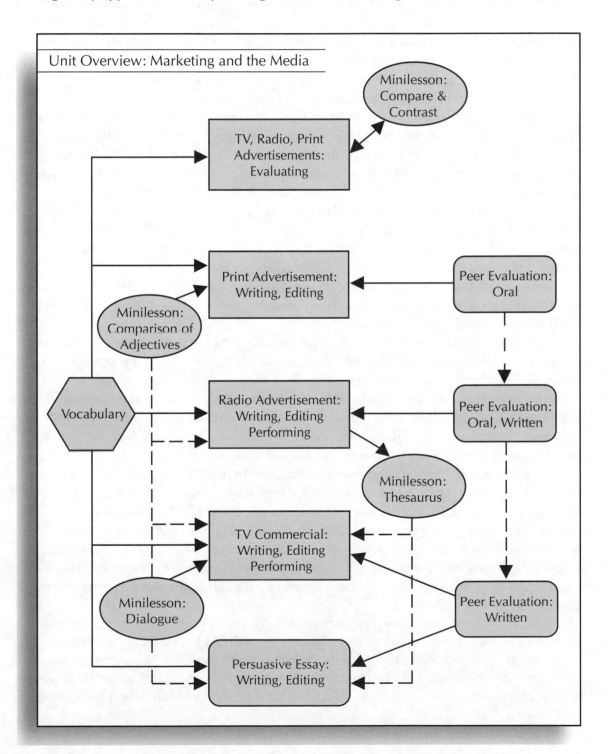

initial planning of units, taking care to include all the standards over the course of the academic year. For example, in developing this set of lessons, I started with the ESL standards and a general idea of the activities I wanted to implement in the unit. I compared the proposed activities with the standards, and if an activity did not align with a standard, I reconsidered its value. In some cases, I rewrote the activity, and in others, the activity was discarded. This helped me eliminate tasks that were vague in focus and therefore of limited value. It also helped direct the activities to skills that were easily transferable to all academic content areas and to real-life situations.

My school district adopted New Standards in 1997. ESOL students were initially exempted from the language arts standards, but students who exited my class were placed directly in language arts classes that were standards based. It quickly became evident that ESOL students had to have knowledge of and experience with standards in order to facilitate their move to mainstream language arts classes. The New Standards requirements, however, were beyond the language abilities of most ESOL students. Accordingly, I have used the TESOL standards to familiarize them with the concept of standards as well as to evaluate their progress in English acquisition.

The ESL standards and the New Standards performance objectives, respectively, are written with different student populations in mind. Although presented in dissimilar language, they do interact to some degree. For example, both require that students compare and contrast, ask and answer questions, and use contextual clues. In preparing units, I have used those elements of the New Standards that are most closely aligned with the ESL standards. Although the ESL standards remain central, the nature of some assignments, such as the persuasive essay, is influenced by New Standards requirements. A core assignment reflecting New Standards requirements is part of each marking period. For these, I follow the same procedures used in mainstream English language arts classes: process writing, rubric design, required achievement of standards, provision of extra time to meet standards. As always, assignments of this nature are assessed taking each student's language level into account.

When we first began, many of my students were very uncomfortable with the idea of standards. I made goal and standard posters that were displayed in the classroom for quick student reference. These also gave students the opportunity to evaluate themselves on an ongoing basis and to seek clarification when needed. As we worked through the activities in this unit, I found that students' attitudes toward standards improved. The consistent language of the ESL progress indicators provided clear-cut objectives and a set of practical skills on which to base course activities and assessments.

Rubrics are the basis of most formal assessment in my class. The ESL standards make rubric design easier by specifying concrete, observable, language-related behavior, with progress indicators that are easy for students to comprehend. I use several types of rubrics, beginning with a simple one based on assigned points, and then graduating to the New Standards type used in mainstream English language arts classrooms. In my class, I also frequently use peer evaluations, which help students focus on the skills they need to develop. Students become more aware of the goals and standards by observing them in the work of others.

I have a master chart for every unit, focusing on those standards to be assessed. This chart is kept in my seating chart folder, where it is readily available. Students are expected to achieve 80% of the progress indicators on this chart, as suggested in *Scenarios for ESL Standards-Based Assessment* (TESOL, in press). Students who do not reach that level receive additional help in the after-school tutoring session, where we can work one-on-one.

I also maintain a Standards Chart for each student, like the one shown for this unit.

Standards Chart

Persuasive Writing

Student Name _____

	Date	Date	Date	Date	Date
Introduction: 1.1, 2.1					
Engage listener's attention					
Volunteer information, respond to Qs					
Elicit information, ask clarification Qs					
Clarify and restate information					
Take turns in a group					
Ask a teacher to restate or simplify					
Join in a group response					
Follow directions to form groups					
TV & Radio Ads: 3.1, 3.2					
Identify language used in commercials					
Analyze nonverbal behavior					
Describe intent, focusing on nonverbal					
Print Ads: 1.2					
Read and respond to print ads					
Creating Print Ads: 2.2, 3.1					
Gather and organize materials					
Construct a graphic					
Edit and revise own assignments					
Synthesize, analyze, evaluate					
Create a commercial					
Creating Radio Ads: 2.2					
Synthesize, analyze, evaluate					
Take a position and support it					
Edit and revise own assignments					
Creating TV Commercials: 3.1, 3.2					
Advise peers on appropriate language					
Create a commercial					
Maintain appropriate eye contact					
Add gestures to correspond to dialogue					
Analyze nonverbal behavior					
Persuasive Essay: 2.2					
Edit and revise own assignment					
Take a position and support it					

Comments:

I make entries on the chart at the end of a unit. The charts are kept in the students' portfolios, where students can check them to see the areas in which progress has been made and the areas in which work must be done. The students and I evaluate the whole portfolio once per marking period. This is done individually, then together. By examining charts on an ongoing basis, I can identify skills that need to be taught, reviewed, clarified, or reinforced.

Activities

Introducing Persuasive Language

We began this unit with a lesson that introduced the concept of persuasion and the vocabulary associated with it. I used students' own experiences by having them fill in a questionnaire relating their experiences to the concept of persuasion. The second segment of the lesson consisted of a vocabulary sheet.

Goal 1, Standard 1 **To use English to communicate in social settings: Students will use English to participate in social interactions.**

Descriptors
- sharing and requesting information
- engaging in conversation

Progress Indicators
- engage listeners' attention verbally or nonverbally
- volunteer information and respond to questions about self and family
- elicit information and ask clarification questions
- clarify and restate information as needed

Goal 2, Standard 1 **To use English to achieve academically in all content areas: Students will use English to interact in the classroom.**

Descriptors
- following oral and written directions, implicit and explicit
- requesting and providing clarification
- participating in full-class, group, and pair discussions
- asking and answering questions

Progress Indicators
- take turns when speaking in a group
- ask a teacher to restate or simplify directions
- join in a group response at the appropriate time
- follow directions to form groups

Questionnaire

Persuasive Writing

Read each set of questions carefully. Answer each question according to your own experience.

1. Have you ever tried to get your mom or dad to take you somewhere he/she did not want to go? (Where?)
   Were you successful?
   How did you get him/her to do it? What did you say?

2. Have you ever tried to get a friend/brother/sister to lend you something? (What?)
   Were you successful?
   How did you get him/her to lend it? What did you say?

3. Have you ever done something for a friend or relative that you didn't really want to do? (What?)
   How did that person get you to do it?

Read over your answers. What worked? What did not work? Why/why not? (You do not have to write your answers, but be prepared to discuss them!)

PROCEDURE

- Each student received a copy of the questionnaire shown above. They were asked to describe their experiences getting others to do something and to tell how they did it. When all students were finished, I asked them to choose a partner and share their responses with one another.

- We then shared our answers as a class, recording responses on the board for clarification and consideration. We examined their *how* lists in detail, evaluating each answer for strength and success. I explained that each of them had just shared at least one situation in which they had attempted to use a form of persuasion and that their *hows* were in reality supporting arguments or reasons for their position.

- As a group, we considered the terms *persuasion* and *persuasive*, defining each in our own terms. Each student then received a short vocabulary sheet, which was duplicated on a wall poster (see p. 92). After reviewing the pronunciation of each term, I explained that these were all words that they would hear repeatedly during our unit. We defined most of these terms, consulting the dictionary only when no one could provide a satisfactory meaning.

- This portion of the lesson finished with a quick brainstorming session on synonyms for *persuade*. Students added these terms to their own lists as I added them to the unit vocabulary poster.

Unit Vocabulary

persuade	*advertisement*
persuasive	*jingle*
persuasion	*argument* (two meanings)
copy (three meanings)	*opinion*
reason	*commercial*
support	*graphic*

ASSESSMENT

All students were expected to participate in the discussions. Students who answered appropriately, using correct English, received an oral point. These were recorded on the class seating chart under each student's name. In addition, I checked off the appropriate box on my standards chart.

Comparing and Contrasting Television and Radio Advertisements

To familiarize students with the concept of advertising, I began this lesson with television commercials, something everyone had experienced. I wanted the class to see how advertising is presented and how advertisements use language effectively. By also using radio advertisements, students were able to make the connection between nonverbal cues such as tone and intonation and the effectiveness of language. The purely oral aspect of the radio commercials also allowed students to consider the importance of the contextual clues that we all take from facial expressions and gestures.

One way I evaluate students is by requiring that they earn oral points. Students earn the equivalent of a quiz grade through class participation, with adjustments made each quarter for lost classes, reading- and writing-only classes, and absences. This allows a quick check at any point on the student's achievement. It is also a quick way to check on listening comprehension. A student with few points may not understand what is being asked or discussed. I can then work with that student individually.

Goal 3, Standard 1   To use English in socially and culturally appropriate ways: Students will use the appropriate language variety, register, and genre according to audience, purpose, and setting.

Descriptors

- using the appropriate degree of formality with different audiences and settings

- responding to slang, idioms, and humor appropriately

Progress Indicator

- identify how language is used in commercials

Goal 3, Standard 2 To use English in socially and culturally appropriate ways: Students will use nonverbal communication appropriate to audience, purpose, and setting.

Descriptors

- responding appropriately to nonverbal cues and body language
- recognizing and adjusting behavior in response to nonverbal cues

Progress Indicators

- analyze nonverbal behavior
- describe intent by focusing on nonverbal behavior in commercials

PROCEDURE

- I explained that we were going to view or listen to a number of different advertisements on television and radio and examine them for five different features, recording our observations on the worksheet provided. Before having the students do this, I modeled a possible answer, writing it on the board.

- Students had to complete the worksheet for themselves, but they were permitted to work in pairs or small groups if they found this more effective. We viewed three commercials, then paused to complete the observation notes. We followed the same procedure with the radio commercials. Throughout this time, I was available for help. One student's completed worksheet is shown on page 94.

- In small groups, students used the back of the worksheet to draw and complete a **Venn diagram** based on their observations. They shared their responses by writing them on the blackboard. The final worksheet question was the basis for further classroom discussion. Completed worksheets were collected for future reference.

If your classroom is not cable-ready, you might assign this as homework. You could assign a time and channel for everyone to watch, with specific instructions to rate the first three commercials that appear. You could also record the commercials beforehand and play them back on a VCR.

My classes are seldom composed of students at the same ESL level, so I need to use activities that are effective for and adaptable to all levels. Class seating allows a range of language abilities at every grouping, giving lower proficiency students stronger language models. Grouping for activities usually follows this seating arrangement, although I allow students to select their own partner(s) at least once per quarter. Assigned seats change twice per quarter. Through the course of the academic year, each student works with nearly every classmate.

Completed Worksheet

Persuasive Writing Unit: TV/ Radio Ads Worksheet
Listen and watch each commercial. Complete the chart for each commercial.

CommercialProduct	Song/jingle?	Action ?	Words?	Most influence?
cheerios	background only	cereal + spoon	reduce cancert heardisea	word
Benecol Salad dressing	no	Pincinic guest orries	reduce cholesterd	action
Sprint cellurar Phone	mysterou music	2 men detectives	cheaper internet in my hand	music words

Now listen to the radio ads and complete the same information.*

Product	Song/jingle	*Word Choices?	words	Most influence
Chrysler	noise of cars	Poor content couldent Understand (to fast)		Nothing
Clinton car + Truck	sweet music	good	You dont have to take my word for it	words properly said clear
Picca Hut	music lively	good	meat its a guy pizza	words had effect imagine product

On the back, draw and complete a VENN diagram for tv and radio ads.

In which type of ad were the words most important ? Explain your answer.

- I took this opportunity to contrast U.S. media and business practices with those of students' home countries. This led to a discussion on the value of watching television and control of television by government.

ASSESSMENT

The completed worksheet and class discussion were used to gauge the students' understanding. The progress indicators that were achieved were

Everyone had a strong opinion to present. Of particular interest were differences in the material that could be broadcast. One girl was surprised that serious government procedures such as the 1999 presidential impeachment hearings had been broadcast live because this would not have been tolerated in her country. We also learned that all of the students watched television, but the boys tended to watch the Discovery Channel and the Learning Channel, whereas most of the girls preferred soap operas in their primary language.

credited on the unit master list. I gave credit in my grade book for completion of the worksheet. Examining these worksheets gave me additional information. Although few students had trouble with the television commercials, a number of them found the radio advertisements difficult to follow. When asked about this, most of them replied, "They talked too fast," or "I didn't really know what they were selling." This not only fed into a later activity (the radio advertisement), but also impressed upon them the need to be clear in their speech. It also reminded me that second language learners may need more visual support and that the normal rate of speech may be too fast for them. I noted for further monitoring those students who had difficulty and relayed the information to their content area teachers.

Reading and Evaluating Print Advertisements

The purpose of this lesson was to reinforce what had already been taught, particularly vocabulary, and to introduce the concept of audience. I also wanted to expose my students to a greater variety of printed material. The periodicals they read were primarily youth-oriented "fanzines" about recording artists, actors, or professional wrestlers. I provided a wider choice, including news, sports, women's, food, celebrity, and general interest magazines.

Goal 1, Standard 2 **To use English to communicate in social settings: Students interact in, through, and with spoken and written English for personal expression and enjoyment.**

Descriptors

- expressing personal needs, feelings, and ideas
- participating in popular culture

Progress Indicator

- read and respond to print advertisements

PROCEDURE

- I showed two advertisements to the class and asked them to identify the copy, headline, and graphic in each. I chose one of the popular milk ads and an ad for a national brand of makeup. First I pointed to a part of the ad, elicited which vocabulary word students would use to explain it, and, if appropriate, asked a student to read that section for the class. We then reversed the process, with students pointing out the section of the advertisement as I supplied the term.

- I explained that we were going to add a new term to our vocabulary. I asked them to indicate by a show of hands if they had seen a movie, a concert, a play, or a television show. Everybody in the class had. The students were asked to give the term that referred to people seeing these performances. I explained that *audience* also applies to written language, and we added the word and its definition to our vocabulary list.

- Examining each advertisement individually, students had to explain what was being sold and to whom. They considered what specific features in each ad targeted a certain audience, whether it was the graphic, the copy, or a combination of these.

- In cooperative groups, students selected three different magazines, then four specific ads per magazine. They noted if a graphic was used and described it. They then identified the audience as they perceived it: children, teens, women, and so on. For the "words" category, I asked them to look for lively language and comparative language, writing down any words that they found particularly good. Finally, they had to decide and indicate, with a simple yes or no, whether or not they felt the entire ad was effective. After finishing this, each group shared its findings with the other groups, using the terms we had learned and providing reasons for their decisions. One group's completed survey is shown.

Completed Survey

Persuasive Writing Unit: Print Ad Survey

Choose 3 different magazines. In each magazine, you will locate 4 different ads. Complete the chart using the ads.

Magazine?	Product?	Graphic?	Audience?	Words?	Effective?
1. people	cosmetics (olay)	woman-lips fingers	woman (30's+	"feel special"	yes
2. Readers Digest	nike	waker	teenagers 13-20	"feel good"	yes
3. News week	computer	colers	911	"thrill of surfing"	yes
4. Readers' Digest	dodge	cartoon	(18+)	"adventure"	yes
5. News week	old mobile	cartoon	18+1	"just more magical"	yes
6.					
7. News week	suzuki	mud	20+40	"mud baths"	yes
8.					
9. cooking	solar	woman	any Age	"True to life"	yes
10. cooking	Cal Burst	Heart	Any Age	"This is calcium"	yes
11. cooking	snack wells	Person Eating	Any Age	"you've never tasted"	yes
12. cooking	Grill mates	Beef	Any Age	"right"	yes
News week	celica	car	21+23	reason	yes

Which ads appealed most to you? Why?
The ads - because of the photographs

Which ads did not interest you? Why not?
The snack wells because the woman looks bad eating it.

Were you influenced more by what you saw (the picture/graphic) or by what you read?
The picture because how it looks makes it clearer

Did you find different ads for the same product? If so, how were they different?
different ads showed different people actions

Why do you think these ads were presented in different ways?
For Different age groups

ASSESSMENT

I observed all groups during the course of the class to make certain all were participating. I checked off the appropriate progress indicator block on my master chart. Students also received classwork credit for successfully completing the worksheet.

Creating Print Advertisements

Creating their own print advertisements required students to produce appropriate persuasive language in a limited fashion. As many of my students had demonstrated artistic talent, I used this as an integral part of this activity. It proved to be a good choice for all my students, particularly those with lower language and academic levels. The activity also provided an opportunity to review comparison of adjectives, a language point often needing reinforcement.

Goal 2, Standard 2   To use English to achieve academically in all content areas: Students will use English to obtain, process, construct, and provide subject matter information in spoken and written form.

Descriptors

- responding to the work of peers and others
- representing information visually and interpreting information presented visually

Progress Indicators

- gather and organize the appropriate materials needed to complete a task
- construct a graphic relating to written form
- edit and revise own written assignments
- synthesize, analyze, and evaluate information

Goal 3, Standard 1   To use English in socially and culturally appropriate ways: Students will use the appropriate language variety, register, and genre according to audience, purpose, and setting.

Descriptors

- using the appropriate degree of formality with different audiences and settings
- using a variety of writing styles appropriate for different audiences, purposes, and settings

Progress Indicator

- create a commercial using an appropriate language style for the product

PROCEDURE

- We began with a review minilesson on the comparison of adjectives. Students were responsible for explaining the patterns used with each of 10 adjectives I supplied, including the irregular adjectives *good* and *bad*. Each student then formulated two questions for the other students to answer, with each question requiring some form of comparison in its answer.

- I told the class that they were going to produce their own individual print advertisements and create an appropriate graphic to accompany their copy. They would be devising an ad for a new soft drink. Each student received a rubric with the specifics of the assignment (see below). We read over it together, clarifying when necessary. A modified form of **process writing** was used to

I try to ensure the success of special needs students by incorporating a variety of activities (e.g., performances, art work, checklists) and by including partner and group work. Using rubrics is also effective for accommodating slower students. Point values may be distributed differently, depending upon languages and academic levels: A rubric might include 30 points for correct spelling, putting a dyslexic student at a clear disadvantage. Assigning 10 or 15 points for spelling gives the student more of an opportunity to succeed. I keep these individualized rubrics in the same basic form as all of the others to protect the student's privacy.

Soft Drink Print Ad Rubric

COPY (60 pts.)

_____ sentence form

_____ correct spelling

_____ descriptive language (at least two adjectives)

_____ appropriate language

_____ correct punctuation and capitalization

_____ understanding of persuasive writing shown

ILLUSTRATION (20 pts.)

_____ is an appropriate size (5)

_____ is colorful and attractive (5)

_____ fits product (10)

GENERAL (20 pts.)

_____ neatness

_____ edit and revise assignment

COMMENTS:

Soda Word Web

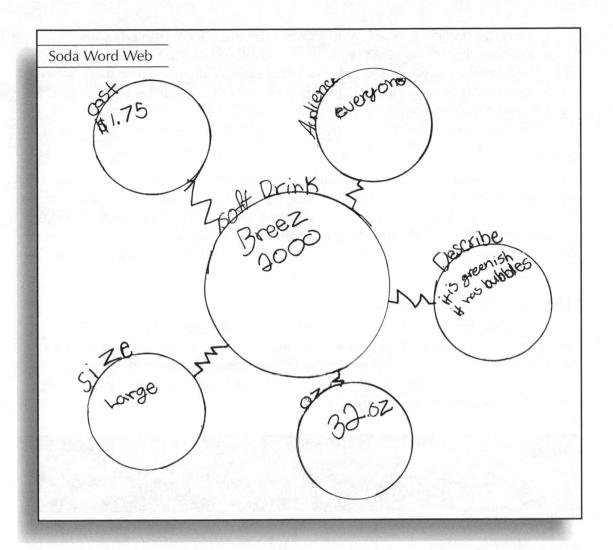

create the advertisements, with no peer or teacher conferences required. All steps were submitted and checked according to the rubric.

- Students began by individually brainstorming the characteristics of their product, then using a word web to complete their ideas. One student's "Soda Word Web" is shown above. They also chose their target audience from one of four suggested groups.

- Using the rubric as a guideline, each student produced a first draft and had a peer read over and comment on it. The peer reviewer then signed this draft. The student and I reviewed subsequent copy together on an informal basis. Although they were working individually, the students were able to test out ideas on one another and seek help if needed.

- After composing the copy, each student devised a graphic to accompany it—a logo, picture, chart, or graph—keeping in mind the

Organization is an ongoing problem for most of my students. When we work on a unit, I give each a large manila envelope in which to keep all of the papers for the unit. The writing activities, with related checklists, forms, and drafts, are then submitted in the envelope.

proposed audience. A final product was submitted, accompanied by all previous drafts. The advertisements were displayed on the bulletin board, with no names visible. Students reacted to them, orally evaluating the relationship between graphic and copy, the effectiveness of the ad in relation to its intended audience, and its overall effective use of language, including comparison of adjectives.

ASSESSMENT

The rubric served as the primary assessment tool. This rubric included progress indicators related to the ESL standards, which were assigned points in the same way as other requirements. I checked off the progress indicator blocks on my master chart. The class discussion provided another opportunity to observe the students' skills, especially their ability to respond appropriately to the work of others, which we had been practicing throughout the year.

Creating Radio Advertisements

I wanted my students to understand how precision in language use becomes more important when it is unaccompanied by any visual clues. By creating radio advertisements, students had to rely solely on their words and the manner in which they delivered them, emphasizing the need for clear and vivid language. This activity also provided an opportunity to introduce the thesaurus.

> **Goal 2, Standard 2** To use English to achieve academically in all content areas: Students will use English to obtain, process, construct, and provide subject matter information in spoken and written form.
>
> ### Descriptors
> - persuading, arguing, negotiating, evaluating, and justifying
> - selecting, connecting, and explaining information
> - responding to the work of peers and others
>
> ### Progress Indicators
> - synthesize, analyze, and evaluate information
> - take a position and support it orally or in writing
> - edit and revise own written assignments

PROCEDURE

- We recalled and described some of the radio ads we had listened to as a class, as well as other advertisements students had heard. We discussed what made an advertisement good or bad.
- For a minilesson on the thesaurus, I played a tape of a very basic radio advertisement I had made, using common words with very general meanings to depict my product. After listening, students were asked to describe as specifically as possible the product I was selling. I asked a series of questions based on their responses. When the students found that they

really could not satisfactorily answer these questions, we considered why. I explained that, although I had used proper and appropriate English, my word choices were not as good as they could have been. I then showed them the thesaurus and explained how it worked. As a group, we sought alternative words for *big* and *different,* making certain to cross-check the options. To provide additional practice, we selected five more overused terms and found other possible choices by using the thesaurus.

In our discussion of good and bad advertisements, students described ads for stores, cars, movies, and the local amusement park. Everyone agreed that ads with music were best and that slogans were good because they are short and easy to remember. Including information on special deals rated highly, as did giving clear directions to the store. Everyone appreciated the repetition of the store or product name. The chief complaint was that an ad was too fast. For example, in ads for cars, many dealers crammed in too much information too quickly. No one liked jingles that withheld the name of the product. They all wanted the ad to be obviously an ad. One student complained, "I just thought it was a bad song."

- I distributed the radio commercial rubric (below), explaining to students that their job was to come up with an advertisement for a fast food restaurant's new sandwich. We read over the rubric, and I explained each item.

- Students employed modified process writing, with no peer or teacher conferences required, to create their advertisements. Although it was not required, students were encouraged to try out their ads on one or two classmates before finalizing their work.

- After composing the commercial, students recorded their advertisements outside of class time, and the ads were later played in class. This eliminated

---

Radio Commercial Rubric

You will write and record your own radio commercial. Your commercial will be about a new sandwich featured at a nationally known fast food restaurant.

You will:

_____ speak in a clear voice (10)

_____ use complete sentences (20)

_____ use colorful words (thesaurus!) (20)

_____ describe your product's characteristics (20)
        (e.g., name, ingredients, size, taste, cost)

_____ use your voice to hold your listener's attention (5)

_____ have an interesting beginning (10)

_____ respond to the work of others (5)

_____ receive a peer score (5)

the element of nervousness inherent in performing before friends and classmates, and, with no visual cues, it focused the audience's attention on the language used.

ASSESSMENT

This assessment had two components. We played the completed tape in class, repeating each advertisement several times. Students rated the various elements of each commercial from 1 (low) to 5 (high) (see below). We then tabulated the results for each ad, averaging scores. All students were encouraged to explain or to support their scoring. The averaged score was added to my scoring on the rubric.

I scored each advertisement using the rubric and credited on my master chart the progress indicators achieved. The span of points on the rubric provided both the students and me with an idea of strengths and weaknesses, which I discussed with each student individually. Some students had difficulty with the editing and revision process. I noted that, in the future, the proofreading/editing checklists should be available at all times.

Creating Television Commercials

I chose television commercials as one of two major projects in this unit because they were something everyone was familiar with. They provided an opportunity to combine written language, the concept of audience, and aspects of nonverbal communication such as tone, volume, stress, intonation, and body language. I found the nonverbal components to be especially important, as many of my students did not use them appropriately. We also reviewed and employed dialogue writing as the language focus.

PROCEDURE

- We had studied dialogue writing earlier in the year, so for review, we engaged in a minilesson on writing dialogue. I selected four students as they entered the class, giving each an index card that defined the student's role in the demonstration to follow. Two were instructed to conduct a short conversation concerning what they had done the night before; the other two were designated as recorders, each writing on the board what one of the speakers related. This provided a sample that we then analyzed. The class discussed the dialogue written on the board and the form in which it was written, noting particularly the lack of complete sentences. This discussion also included when and why one would use dialogue rather than narrative form.

Peer Evaluation for Radio Advertisement

Rate 1 (low) to 5 (high)

_____ Your advertisement grabbed and held my attention.

_____ You spoke in an appropriate tone and at an understandable speed.

_____ You did not overuse common words.

_____ Your word choices helped me "see" your product.

Goal 3, Standard 1 To use English in socially and culturally appropriate ways: Students will use appropriate language variety, register, and genre according to audience, purpose, and setting.

Descriptors

- using the appropriate degree of formality with different audiences and settings
- using a variety of writing styles appropriate for different audiences, purposes, and settings

Progress Indicators

- advise peers on appropriate language use
- create a commercial using an appropriate language style for the product

Goal 3, Standard 2 To use English in socially and culturally appropriate ways: Students will use nonverbal communication appropriate to audience, purpose, and setting.

Descriptors

- interpreting and responding appropriately to nonverbal cues and body language
- using acceptable tone, volume, stress, and intonation in various social settings

Progress Indicators

- maintain appropriate level of eye contact with audience while giving an oral presentation
- add gestures to correspond to a dialogue
- analyze nonverbal behavior

- I then divided the class into small groups, providing them with **dialogue cards**. These cards, used to create short conversations, contained the same setting and topic, but different audiences. After the groups prepared their presentations, they performed before the whole class. To finish the lesson, I asked the students to identify the target audiences. The class discussed how the dialogues were different and why. I based assessment of this minilesson solely on the progress indicators on my master list.

- To create a television commercial, we began by recalling the commercials we had seen, using the worksheets we had completed when we viewed them. On the board, we noted some of the features—jingles and music, use of comparative adjectives, lively language, nonverbal cues.

TV Ad Web

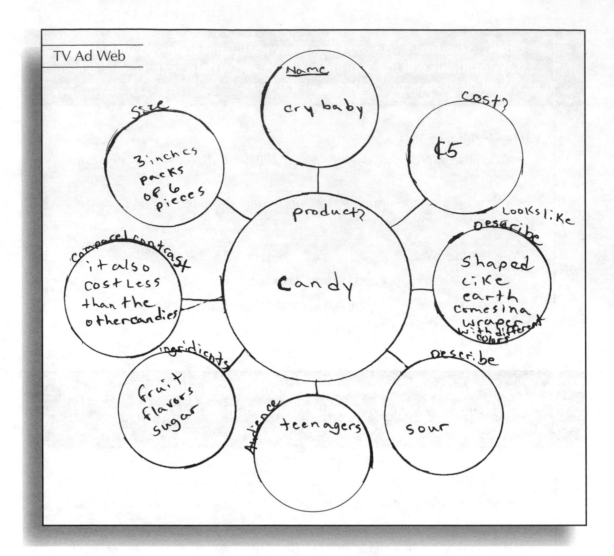

- I explained that we were going to make our own television commercials. Students were allowed to choose a partner (or partners) with whom they wished to work; groups were limited to a maximum of four individuals. In this case, I did not assign a particular product as the subject of these commercials. Students created their own products, and I was available to help anyone who had difficulty making a decision. Each group appointed a secretary whose job it was to record all ideas. A class period was provided for prewriting, based on a word web. One group's completed "TV Ad Web" is shown. I collected these at the end of the period, checking for proper direction and completion.

- Before the students began their actual writing, we reviewed the concept of dialogue and noted that, in order to mimic real-life speech, we would not have to write in complete sentences. The groups followed process writing to compose their commercials. In place of our normal peer conference, students selected another group to listen to and to view their preliminary work. The viewers critiqued this performance using a chart based upon the standards to be assessed.

- Subsequent drafts were written, with one draft being submitted to me for review of language use, grammar, mechanics, and content; I also viewed the accompanying performance. For the teacher conference on this draft, I

Television Commercial Peer Conference

Rate 1 (low) to 5 (high)

_____ You use language that is appropriate for the product and audience.

_____ Your tone and intonation are appropriate.

_____ You make eye contact with others.

_____ Your gestures make sense.

_____ Your commercial shows you know your target audience.

---

made notes concerning written work and performance on their drafts, and we went over them together. Each student received a copy of my evaluation. This permitted the students to ask questions and to clarify or explain their choices to me. They then completed revisions and editing before taping. They had the option to film during class or after school.

- After recording, students viewed their work on the VCR. If dissatisfied, they were able to discuss changes among themselves and to film again. In addition to the final taped performance, students submitted, as a group, all work related to their performance, from the prewriting activity through the final draft.

> When many of my students first came to my class, they did not understand the process of writing and were simply recopying first drafts. I had to teach them the process and constantly reinforce it. I now always collect all portions of writing assignments to make certain that process writing is being followed. I check drafts for revisions, particularly for changes based on peer and teacher feedback.

ASSESSMENT

I used a multipart assessment for the commercials, incorporating written form, performance, and peer evaluation. I graded the written form according to the applicable criteria, shown on page 106, in "Television Commercial Rubric," which included the relevant progress indicators. They had to meet 80% of the criteria accurately to fulfill the New Standards directives, all of which were on my master chart. The class viewed the videotape of all the commercials, and each student completed a peer assessment chart, which was the same as for the peer conference (see above). These were averaged and the peer scores were included on the rubric. In addition, students were encouraged to comment on individual performances as they viewed them.

Persuasive Essay

I completed the unit on persuasive writing with an essay. This served as the core assignment called for by New Standards and as a challenging final writing activity. All of the previous activities were designed with this activity in mind. The essay was a more sophisticated form of persuasion, employing many of the language skills we had studied through advertisements. In keeping with the concept of the media, the essays took the

Television Commercial Rubric

Persuasive Writing

You will prepare a television commercial for presentation to the entire class. Your commercial will show that you understand the idea behind advertising: to persuade people to buy your product. You may work alone, with a partner, or with a group of no more than four. It must be understood that ALL group members are expected to work together and to participate equally in the writing and presentation.

You will

_____ make up a product of your own, including an original brand name (5)

_____ have an interesting introduction to your product (5)

_____ have a slogan, motto, or jingle to sell your product (5)

_____ explain why your product is unique (5)

_____ make your presentation to a target audience (10)

_____ describe your product, using at least five different adjectives and three different adjective forms (10)

_____ use your vocal register and intonation as part of your selling technique (10)

_____ use appropriate gestures (10)

_____ work cooperatively with your partner or group (10)

_____ maintain correct eye contact with actors/audience (10)

_____ use writing process (15)

_____ receive a peer evaluation (5)

form of newspaper editorials. I was primarily interested in the use of support sentences and the development of multiple paragraphs concentrating on one theme, two areas in which my students continued to have difficulty.

Goal 2, Standard 2   To use English to achieve academically in all content areas: Students will use English to obtain, process, and provide subject matter information in spoken and written form.

Descriptor
- persuading, arguing, negotiating, evaluating, and justifying

Progress Indicators
- edit and revise own written assignment
- take a position and support it orally or in writing

PROCEDURE

- To make certain that everyone understood what an editorial was, I asked students to locate the editorials in a number of newspapers. I then asked them why newspapers included them. Student responses included "The newspaper talks about something that happened and tells if it is a good or bad thing." "The editor explains why you should vote for someone." "It's where the editor tells you what he wants you to think."

- I provided copies of three editorials to the class, with the topics varying from local issues to international matters. I asked the class to identify the position of the author and the reasons given by the author for that particular position. I reminded them that these reasons served as the support sentences for each paragraph. This led to a brief oral review of sentence types and paragraph construction, with the information coming from the students rather than from me.

- After explaining that we would use all the writing skills we had learned to compose our own editorials, I distributed and reviewed the persuasive essay rubric shown on page 108. I also distributed a list of suggested topics, ranging from school-related to societal issues. Students also had the option of coming up with their own topics, subject to teacher approval.

- Students used process writing to complete their essays, with a minimum requirement of three drafts. Prewriting took the form of a yes/no chart, with students listing reasons in support of their positions as well as counterarguments, which the advanced students used later in an expansion of the assignment.

- After completion of the first draft, students selected another class member to critique their writing. The peer conference form shown on page 109 was used; students were encouraged to discuss their evaluations with the writers as well.

- After making revisions and writing a second draft, students had the required teacher conference. Using the same form as a basis, I met with each student individually, identifying strong areas as well as problems. In addition to the language elements, students were asked to consider their writing style.

- Before submitting their essays, students used the proofreading/editing checklist for a last review. Two versions of this checklist were available, with the student's ESL level determining which was used. Students prepared their final essays on the computer. One student's completed persuasive essay is shown on page 110.

My students represent a broad spectrum of academic levels and a range of English proficiency. The proofreading/editing checklist provides a general outline to guide writing for all students, but also allows for individual needs. I do not expect students to have mastered all the items listed initially. As the year progresses, I add more items to include material we have covered as well as skills that are challenging. The list gives students and me a clearer idea of what areas need improvement. Subsequent checklists incorporate those items on a class and an individual basis.

Persuasive Essay Rubric

Persuasive Writing: Editorial

You will choose a topic for a persuasive essay. This is your core assignment for this quarter. Your essay will be graded on the following:

TO MEET STANDARDS:

_____ write in paragraph form

_____ write in complete sentences

_____ have generally correct mechanics (80%)

_____ provide an interesting topic sentence for each paragraph

_____ provide enough support for each paragraph

_____ use a variety of sentences (simple and compound)

_____ show a general understanding of persuasive writing through language choices

_____ have a clear focus on task, with no irrelevant material

_____ provide adequate content

_____ edit and revise your own assignment

_____ use writing process

_____ explain away weak points/counterarguments (ADVANCED STUDENTS ONLY)

TO EXCEED STANDARDS:

_____ write in paragraph form

_____ write in complete sentences

_____ have correct mechanics (100%)

_____ provide an interesting topic sentence for each paragraph

_____ provide enough support for each paragraph

_____ use a variety of sentences (simple, compound, and complex)

_____ show a general understanding of persuasive writing through language choices

_____ have a clear focus on task, with no irrelevant material

_____ provide adequate content

_____ use varied vocabulary, avoiding overused words and phrases

_____ provide an introduction and closing for your essay

_____ edit and revise your own assignment

_____ use writing process

_____ explain away weak points/counterarguments (ADVANCED STUDENTS ONLY)

Peer Conference Form

Peer Conference for _____

Assignment _____

Done By _____

Date _____

	Peer	Teacher
1. You used end punctuation correctly.	_____	_____
2. You began sentences with a capitalized word.	_____	_____
3. You capitalized words correctly (names, places, etc.)	_____	_____
4. You wrote in complete sentences.	_____	_____
5. You wrote in paragraph form.	_____	_____
6. You did not use run-on sentences.	_____	_____
7. You have a topic sentence for each paragraph.	_____	_____
8. You have enough support sentences in each paragraph.	_____	_____
9. You used the correct verb tense.	_____	_____
10. Your subjects (doers) and verbs (actions) go together.	_____	_____
11. Your writing had a clear focus. (I understood what you wanted to tell me.)	_____	_____
12. Your writing was interesting.	_____	_____

Comments:

Peer:

Author:

Teacher:

Author:

- Advanced students had an additional component in their writing, meant to challenge their abilities. They were instructed to try to "argument-proof" their essay, coming up with reasons why those "no" factors on their original brainstorming chart were invalid. This component was then incorporated into their essay as a separate paragraph. I included this for the advanced students because it was part of the New Standards persuasive essay criteria.

- Although I posted a tentative time line as a guide, students worked at their own pace. The homework assignment for this time was simply to continue working on the essay; a number of students also used the after-school tutoring hour.

Completed Persuasive Essay

Class Size Should Be Smaller

There are more than twenty students in each normal American class. Twenty students talk, and only one teacher teaches the large class. This is a stupid situation. Think about this problem seriously. How can one teacher handle more than twenty students? We have to find a good solution as fast as we can. I will write about my thoughts that can help this problem. I hope this essay can help.

Class size should be smaller. As I said, teachers have no chance to care and to teach everybody. The students who are getting A's or B's on report cards can study very well with teachers, but others are out of the teacher's sight. When we check homework, it takes a lot of time to finish the checking. Teachers have to teach all students successfully, but teachers can not do that. The class time is so short that teachers can not go over with students everything.

Not only in the United States' schools, but all over the world, everybody has to think and try to solve this problem. We have to make an investment in many schools and make more classrooms. There should be more teachers in each classroom. Not too many, just two or three teachers will be fine. For the classes which are on high levels, there should be one or two teachers. For the lower levels, there should be more teachers. Our help will make a difference. If we try, we will see the benefits of our education, and make a better world for us and our offspring. Just remember what I said. This is for your better lives.

ASSESSMENT

Because this was, at its core, a New Standards assignment, the rubric employed was slightly different from previous ones and was developed after consultation with mainstream eighth-grade English language arts teachers. The rubric consisted of two separate but similar lists, one for *meets standards,* the other for *exceeds standards.* Points were not assigned to individual items. In order to achieve either level, students were required to satisfy all criteria; failure to do so resulted in a lower, perhaps unacceptable evaluation. (The exception to this was the mechanics criterion on the *meets standards* list, which was placed at 80% accuracy.)

New Standards require that students reach the *meets* level for core assignments. Therefore, students who did not achieve the requirements were given the opportunity to continue working on their essays. The rubric allowed them to identify those areas in which they needed to work, and I met with them to explain, to clarify, and to answer their questions.

ESL progress indicators were included on the rubric. These were also recorded on the master list for the unit.

Additional Information

The concept of persuasive language could easily be adapted for inclusion in a social studies unit. For example, this particular unit could be incorporated into the study of economics. Persuasion could also be related to the study of government, particularly the election process. During an active campaign season, students could examine and analyze political advertisements, run their own campaigns, give speeches, and stage a debate. This could be done in conjunction with the social studies teacher or as an ESL unit.

REFERENCES AND RESOURCES

Kemper, D., Sebranek, P., & Meyer, V. (1998). *All write*. Wilmington, MA: Write Source.
  A writing handbook designed with the second language learner in mind, this book is a valuable reference for students.

Jasmine, J. (1992). *Portfolio assessment for your whole language classroom*. Huntington Beach, CA: Teacher Created Materials.
  This book provides explanations of various portfolio assessments and includes blackline masters for use by teacher and student.

National Center on Education and the Economy. (1998). *Performance standards: Vol. 2. Middle school*. Washington, DC: Author.

TESOL. (1997). *ESL standards for pre-K–12 students*. Alexandria, VA: Author.

TESOL. (in press). *Scenarios for ESL standards-based assessment*. Alexandria, VA: Author.

UNIT 5
Exploring How We Live: Community

OLGA RYZHIKOV

Introduction

You cannot imagine what happened in my dream! That's the most exciting, wonderful, and weird dream I have ever had before! That night I went to bed really late, because I talked to my friend about Renaissance. We study it in my world studies class. All of a sudden I saw a huge blue hand . . . . When the hand got on my bed, I was shocked and petrified. A second later the blue hand spoke, "Hi, Wei! Don't be scared, I won't hurt you. People call me Journey Train. Tonight I am going to take you to a magic place . . . ." Soon, he brought me to a place I had never seen before. The floor was all white just as if I was standing above clouds. In front of me was a huge book . . . . The book was open and there was a mirror in it and on the mirror there were about thousand choices. So I read all the choices all over again, and then I chose . . .

Thus began a letter written by Wei, a seventh-grade ESOL student. To find out why Journey Train visited Wei and where he took her after she had made her choice in the magic book, I invite you to our middle school ESL classroom, where sixth, seventh, and eighth graders are preparing to start their journey into the theme of community. (The student names given in this unit are real and used with permission.)

Context

Grade levels: Sixth, seventh, and eighth grades

English proficiency level: Intermediate

Native languages of students: Mixed; predominantly Spanish, Bengali, French, Chinese, Russian

Focus of instruction: ESL, social studies, language arts

Type of class: ESL class, one period a day

Length of unit: 9 weeks

Unit Overview

"Community" is the second of four units in the new intermediate ESL curriculum recently adopted systemwide in Montgomery County (Daddone et al., 1998; see Short, 2000, for a description of the development of this curriculum and its alignment with the ESL standards and the district English language arts standards). This theme, which explores old and new communities, is a natural continuation of the first unit, where students focused on their cultural roots, their own immigration stories, and their hopes and dreams for the future. By providing a framework for teaching language in a context that is meaningful and interesting for middle school students, these units help them adapt to their new culture as they develop important academic skills. To further ensure their success in mainstream classes, each unit in the intermediate curriculum includes interdisciplinary connections that help students learn important academic content while improving their English. This unit has ample opportunities to connect English language learning with social studies.

In this unit, I want my students to learn about the past and present of the new country they now call home. I hope to bridge the background knowledge gap that exists between native speakers, who have heard and read stories about their country all their lives, and my ESOL students, most of whom lack any background knowledge about the United States, and some of whom have very little knowledge of the world in general. This lack of background knowledge makes it difficult for ESOL students to succeed in their social studies classes. My students often tell me how hard it is for them to understand what their social studies teacher is talking about. The problem is definitely not only language but also the absence of background knowledge that students can build on to acquire new information. By tapping into students' natural curiosity and creativity, the theme of community can make history relevant and accessible.

The unit's activities are designed to enable students to

- explore and identify the elements that make up a community
- use different sources to research the colonial period of U.S. history
- use acquired information to write an essay comparing life in America now and in colonial times
- use different sources to research a typical community of the time period studied in their mainstream social studies class
- write a friendly letter about an imaginary trip to an ancient land
- increase their command of English grammar and vocabulary through daily language minilessons related to unit activities
- read American folktales to explore community values
- create their own ideal community

The unit overview shows how the various kinds of activities relate to each other.

Standards

When a group of middle and high school ESL teachers first started working on the new curriculum, we decided on the four major themes around which we wanted to build our curriculum. As we discussed the themes, we kept three goals in mind. We wanted the themes to be

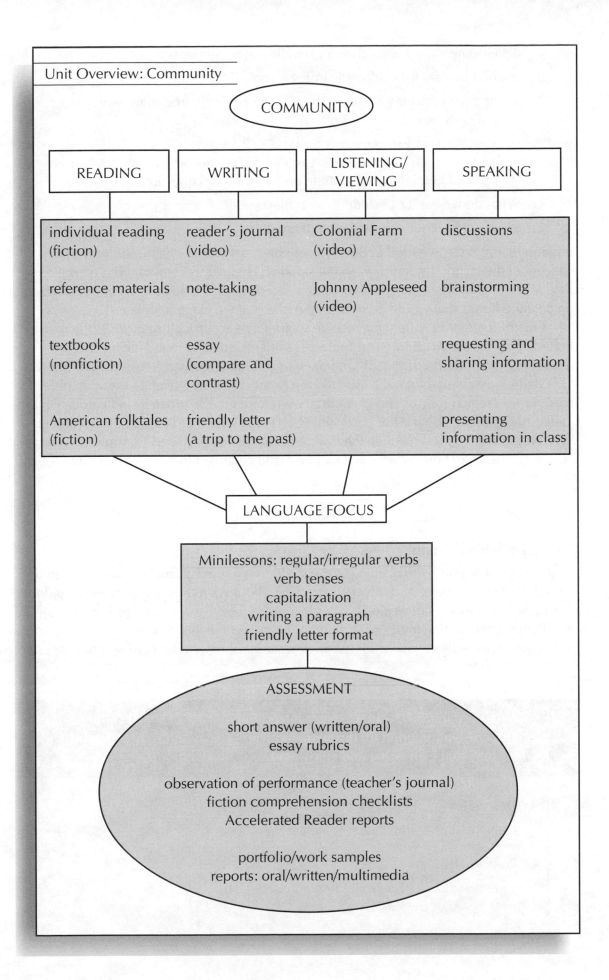

Unit Overview: Community

COMMUNITY

READING	WRITING	LISTENING/ VIEWING	SPEAKING
individual reading (fiction)	reader's journal (video)	Colonial Farm (video)	discussions
reference materials	note-taking	Johnny Appleseed (video)	brainstorming
textbooks (nonfiction)	essay (compare and contrast)		requesting and sharing information
American folktales (fiction)	friendly letter (a trip to the past)		presenting information in class

LANGUAGE FOCUS

Minilessons: regular/irregular verbs
verb tenses
capitalization
writing a paragraph
friendly letter format

ASSESSMENT

short answer (written/oral)
essay rubrics

observation of performance (teacher's journal)
fiction comprehension checklists
Accelerated Reader reports

portfolio/work samples
reports: oral/written/multimedia

1. developmentally appropriate for middle school students

2. cultural bridges for students learning a second language

3. aligned with the new Montgomery County English curriculum, which is thematically based.

Next we concentrated on *ESL Standards for Pre-K–12 Students* (TESOL, 1997). We soon discovered that the format of three goals, each with three accompanying standards, was very easy to use and helped us concentrate on two essential questions:

1. What do we want our students to achieve?

2. What kinds of activities will help them achieve it?

In planning the units, we tried to develop activities that would enable students to achieve all the standards. In this way, the standards helped us keep in mind a broader picture of our students' linguistic and cultural needs. They made us think about developing balanced units that would address all the needs of language learners.

One of the more challenging tasks in writing a new curriculum is developing an ongoing assessment procedure that indicates students' success in achieving the standards. Here both the ESL standards and *Scenarios for ESL Standards-Based Assessment* (TESOL, in press) were of great help. The descriptors were very useful in writing objectives. As we created rubrics and checklists, we referred to the progress indicators, which guided our thinking about what observable behaviors would indicate to us that students were progressing toward meeting the standards. *Scenarios* provided examples of a large variety of assessment procedures that can be readily adapted to other content and contexts.

Activities

Setting Individual Goals

I begin each new unit by explaining to the students what we, as a class, are going to do in the following 9 weeks, and having them think about what they, as learners, would like to achieve. Students become much better learners if they assume responsibility for the learning process. Setting their own unit goals helps them feel in charge of what is going on in class. This is also the time for me to start students' individual reading programs for the unit.

> ***Goal 1, Standard 2*** **To use English to communicate in social settings: Students will interact in, through, and with spoken and written English for personal expression and enjoyment.**
>
> ***Descriptor***
> - expressing personal needs, feelings, and ideas
>
> ***Progress Indicator***
> - discuss issues of personal importance or value

Goal 1, Standard 3   To use English to communicate in social settings; students will use learning strategies to extend their communicative competence.

Descriptor

- self-monitoring and self-evaluating language development

Progress Indicator

- set own goals for reading performance

PROCEDURE

- Before starting this unit, I asked students to reflect on the previous unit and tell me what we had accomplished as a class and individually. We discussed the reading they did in class and at home, the projects they had completed and shared in class, and how much they read in English on their own. I used this as an opportunity for the students to reflect on what they were especially successful in, and what they could have done differently.

- After presenting the new theme, I handed out the unit activities and individual goals worksheet shown. The unit activities written at the top of the page served as a plan of action, informing students what we were going to do. At the same time, the worksheet was a contract with each student for the individual reading they were to do at home and in class during **sustained silent reading (SSR)** time. Students filled in the Individual Goals section, determining for themselves how many pages they would read each day, at what reading levels. Knowing my students' strengths and weaknesses in reading, I helped them set realistic goals. Some students were ready to try more difficult books, and others needed more practice reading at the same level. Students could also add additional goals, such as doing their homework every day, working on their reading speed, or trying new authors or genres.

The Accelerated Reader (AR) Computerized Reading Management Program (1998) tracks students' progress in reading by providing tests for thousands of titles. After reading a book on the AR list, students take a computerized multiple-choice comprehension test. They get reading points based on the difficulty of the book and the number of questions answered correctly. By printing students' reading records showing the number of books read, the number of AR tests passed, and the level of difficulty of the books, AR allows the teacher to track students' progress.

ASSESSMENT

Students stapled their goals to their individual portfolios and used them throughout the unit for self-evaluation of work done and to monitor their progress. I carefully read students' goals to assess their ability to set short-term goals for themselves and reflect on their own abilities and needs.

Unit Activities and Individual Goals

Name _____

Grade _____

Community

UNIT ACTIVITIES

1. Read a minimum of 30 minutes each night.

2. Read selected materials in class.

3. Read and present to class one of the American folk tales.

4. Write an essay comparing life in our community now with life in the past.

5. Write a letter to a friend about an imaginary trip to the past.

6. Create and present an ideal community.

INDIVIDUAL GOALS

1. I will read _____ pages every week.

2. I will try to read on a _____ reading level.

3. My goal is to get _____ AR points and join the _____ club.

4. I will also _____.

Understanding the Concept of Community

As I start any new theme, I like to begin with an activity that will show me how much my students already know about it, and at the same time make it relevant and interesting to them. By asking my students to define the concept of community, I was able to see what background knowledge they had and what I had to introduce.

Goal 1, Standard 3 **To use English to communicate in social settings: Students will use learning strategies to extend their communicative competence.**

Descriptors

- testing hypotheses about language

- seeking support and feedback from others

Progress Indicators

- use a dictionary to validate choice of language

- test appropriate use of new vocabulary, phrases, and structures

> **Goal 2, Standard 1** To use English to achieve academically in all
> content areas: Students will use English to interact in the classroom.

Descriptors

- following oral and written directions
- requesting and providing clarification
- participating in group discussions
- elaborating and extending other people's ideas and thoughts

Progress Indicators

- use polite forms to negotiate and reach consensus
- take turns when speaking
- ask a teacher to restate or simplify directions

PROCEDURE

- I passed out "Community Worksheet," which contained questions about the concept of community (see p. 120). Students were to think about the first three questions individually and then share their thoughts with the class.

- The students were able to define what makes a group of people a community but had trouble thinking more globally. They did not think of community in terms of a country, the world, or all of humankind. Our discussion helped ensure that everybody understood that one can belong to a large number of communities at the same time.

- Students wrote their own definitions of the word *community* and then looked the word up in the dictionary. As they compared the dictionary definition with their own, they were pleased about how close they were.

- We then decided on a class definition of the word *community,* which I wrote on a poster for the bulletin board, and the students wrote on their worksheets.

ASSESSMENT

My assessment of students' background knowledge showed that in developing the theme, I would need to reinforce a global understanding of the term *community.* I also used this activity as an opportunity to observe students' dictionary skills.

Video: *A Colonial Farm*

Using a video to introduce new concepts and vocabulary helps overcome students' limitations in vocabulary and structure and allows discussion of sophisticated topics. When we later encounter new information in written text, we can also make reference to the visual images of the video.

Community Worksheet

Community

1. What makes a group of people a community? List the characteristics of a community.

_____

_____

_____

2. What groups, clubs, and organizations do you belong to?

_____

_____

_____

3. Order the groups you belong to from most important to least important to you.

_____

_____

_____

4. Write your definition of community.

_____

_____

_____

5. Write the class definition of community.

_____

_____

_____

PROCEDURE

- Before watching *A Colonial Farm* (Bowen, 1993), I asked students to discuss in small groups what they thought life was like in our community 200 years ago. They could either list their ideas on paper or draw pictures. One representative from each group then shared the group's conclusions with the whole class.

- Students had copies of "Elements of a Community Worksheet" for taking notes while watching the video (see p. 121). To make sure everyone understood the meanings of the categories listed on the worksheet, I displayed a big poster where each category was illustrated with pictures.

Completing this worksheet helped students learn how to take notes in other classes as well. If they did not know a word in English, they were allowed to write it in their own language or to draw a picture of it. We discussed how it is helpful to use their first language when taking notes. For students who do not write in their native language, drawing pictures can be the first step to note-taking.

Goal 2, Standard 2   To use English to achieve academically in all content areas: Students will use English to obtain, process, construct, and provide subject matter information in spoken and written form.

Descriptors

- listening to information
- gathering information orally and in writing
- selecting, connecting, and retelling information
- understanding and producing vocabulary
- interpreting information presented visually

Progress Indicators

- take notes during a video in order to summarize key concepts
- synthesize, analyze, and evaluate information
- locate information appropriate to the assignment in the video
- record observations

- As students watched the video, they filled in information about the elements of a colonial community. I stopped the video several times to give the students an opportunity to work on their notes.

- After the video, students worked in groups to compare their notes and help each other complete the information. Each group then shared its information with the class.

Elements of a Community Worksheet

Elements of a Community	Notes
Shelter/Buildings	
Clothing	
Transportation	
Everyday Chores/Tasks	
Food/Cooking	
Crops/Animals	
Furniture	
Tools and Equipment	
Education	

ASSESSMENT AND ADDITIONAL ACTIVITY

The completed worksheets allowed me to evaluate achievement of the progress indicators. I also used them to evaluate the vocabulary they had used to describe elements of a community. Based on this assessment, I decided to teach additional vocabulary for describing clothing material and farm chores. For this purpose, I divided the class into two groups, Picasso and Shakespeare. The students who were good at drawing joined the first group and drew pictures illustrating colonists' clothing, chores they had, and other elements of their community. The Shakespeare group collected additional vocabulary, using picture dictionaries, bilingual dictionaries, and the CD-ROM *Language Discoveries* (Applied Optical Media Corporation, 1994). They were responsible for labeling the pictures done by the Picasso group and teaching this vocabulary to the class.

Individualized Reading

The amount of reading students do is an indicator of their future success in a mainstream classroom and in future standardized testing. The more they read, the more vocabulary and structure they learn, and the better writers they become. That is why I encourage my students to read as much as possible both at school and at home. My goals are to have students read as much as they can at an appropriate level of difficulty (different for each student), gradually increase the level of difficulty, and acquire a habit of reading for personal enjoyment. Students' homework every day is to read for 30 minutes, and I include 15 minutes of SSR time in daily instruction.

> *Goal 1, Standard 2* To use English to communicate in social settings: Students will interact in, through, and with spoken and written English for personal expression and enjoyment.
>
> ### Descriptors
> - participating in popular culture
> - participating in a favorite activity
> - expressing personal ideas
>
> ### Progress Indicators
> - recommend a book to a friend
> - write in a reader's journal
> - locate information
> - read stories and books, use computer programs
> - ask information questions for personal reasons
> - make requests for personal reasons
> - talk about a favorite book

PROCEDURE

- As a class, we went to the media center to choose books. Some students already knew how to read the information on the cover of the book and chose according to their interests. Some chose books written by the same authors they had read for the previous unit. Students who were nonreaders in their native languages chose books with pictures, a minimum of text on each page, and a large font. I had taught them to use the Accelerated Reader Program lists and choose books on their reading level, gradually increasing difficulty as they were successful with the tests at a particular level.

Ideally, students would choose books connected with the theme of community, but in a class with many different reading levels, that is difficult to do. I therefore decided not to limit students to the community theme only, and allowed them to choose any book that was appropriate. Whenever possible, I tried to connect our class discussions of communities with their individual readings.

- In the classroom, we had a chart where stickers showed how many books students had read on their own. Comprehension was checked by the

---

Sample Reading Report

```
04/13/99                        Accelerated Reader
                              Student Record Report




                                 Quest    %    Points                  Read
Test   Title                     Rt/Poss  Rt   Earn/Poss  Date         Level
-------------------------------------------------------------------------
 262   Freckle Juice.............  9/10    90   0.9/  1.0  02/02/99     2.0
 349   There's a Boy in the Girls. 9/10    90   5.4/  6.0  02/05/99     4.7
5017   Happy Birthday, Molly!.....  6/10    60   0.6/  1.0  02/16/99     4.1
5227   Kirsten Saves the Day......  9/10    90   0.9/  1.0  02/22/99     3.5
 909   Frankenstein (Longman Clas. 10/10   100   4.0/  4.0  03/17/99     4.0
  72   Ramona and Her Father...... 10/10   100   3.0/  3.0  04/06/99     4.1
 186   Ramona Forever.............  10/10   100   4.0/  4.0  04/13/99     4.1
 304   Beezus and Ramona.........   8/10    80   2.4/  3.0  04/13/99     4.5


                    *** Summary ***
              -----------------------------------
              Average percent correct.....  88.8%
              Average reading level.......  3.9
              Tests taken.................  8
              Tests passed................  8
              Tests failed................  0

              Points possible.............  23.0
              Points earned...............  21.2
              Points used.................   0.0
              Points available............  21.2

              -----------------------------------
```

Great report!

Accelerated Reader Program. When students finished a book, they went to the classroom computer and took the test. If they passed the test, the computer printed a report showing the score, which earned them a sticker on the chart. The report itself went home with words of praise added to it. I wanted my students to share all their successes with their families. One student's sample reading report is shown on page 123.

- I also used another method to monitor reading. Students told me each day what page they were on in their reading books. By comparing the page number from one day to the next, I could say, "I see you did a tremendous amount of work last night!" or "Did you really read for 30 minutes yesterday and read only two pages?" I was immensely pleased when a student said to me, "Yesterday I couldn't put the book down. It was so interesting that I read for 2 hours. I really wanted to finish it!" I knew that student was beginning to read for enjoyment!

- At the end of each month we gave prizes to the three winners of the Accelerated Readers Race. All the students were also reading a lot in order to join one of the AR Clubs: bronze club, for those who got 25–50 AR points, silver for 50–100, and gold for 100 or more. We later added a diamond club for one exceptional reader who got 200 AR points! Pictures of the "members of the club" were placed in the hall under a banner saying "Readers' Hall of Fame." The students also knew that at the end of the grading period, a pizza party or trip to the movie theater would reward the best readers. All these incentives worked, and most of the students started reading on their own.

The game format with elements of competition offered by the Accelerated Reader Program interests my students immediately. They do not feel that they are competing with each other. Rather they see a goal that is in their power to achieve. We always celebrate when we have new "members of the club" and share which particular books helped them achieve their goal. As the year progresses, more and more smiling faces look out proudly from our "Readers' Hall of Fame."

ASSESSMENT

In addition to reading reports, I used response journals and a reading comprehension checklist to assess progress indicators and comprehension. If I noticed from students' response journals that they were struggling with their books, I set up individual conferences to determine what the problem was. I also used parent volunteers who came to my classroom once a week to read individually with students who had problems. Sometimes reading a chapter with somebody else was enough to overcome a difficulty. Other times it was necessary to choose an easier book. I also tried to observe students in the media center as they looked for advice about choosing a book to read, asking their peers and me what the book was about and expressing their enjoyment of and interest in the book they were reading. This gave me an indication of who still needed more help on the difficult road to independent reading.

Writing a Compare and Contrast Essay

Writing helps students acquire English by reinforcing the vocabulary, structure, and idioms they have learned. It allows them to go beyond what has been learned and be adventurous with the language. "The effort to express ideas and the constant use of eye, hand, and brain is a unique way to reinforce learning" (Raimes, 1983, p. 3). In this unit, students write when they take notes, write about what they saw in the video, and write in their reader's journals. They also have three major writing assignments that teach them to write for different purposes, the first of which is a comparative piece.

Goal 2, Standard 2 To use English to achieve academically in all content areas: Students will use English to obtain, process, construct, and provide subject matter information in spoken and written form.

Descriptors

- comparing and contrasting information
- gathering information orally and in writing
- selecting, connecting, and retelling information
- analyzing, synthesizing, and inferring from information
- responding to the work of peers
- persuading, evaluating, and justifying

Progress Indicators

- take notes
- synthesize, analyze, and evaluate information
- locate information appropriate to the assignment
- record observations
- take a position and support it in writing
- define, compare, and classify objects
- edit and revise own written assignments

PROCEDURE

- To prepare students to write a comparative piece, students had to focus on the realities of present-day life in their communities. We did this with the same worksheet that the students had used for taking notes while watching the video. The concept *elements of the community* was reinforced and applied to a new situation. Students also learned the language necessary for describing elements of modern-day Maryland.

- I gave students the worksheet and modeled how to fill it in. As we discussed the first category, students suggested kinds of shelter that could be seen in Maryland now, and I wrote them on an overhead transparency: *apartment houses, single family houses, town houses.* I encouraged students to think about what materials houses are made of and what conveniences are found

Completed Worksheet

Maryland Now

ELEMENTS OF A COMMUNITY	NOTES
Shelter/Buildings Apartments Buildings	single house, townhouses skyscrapers, mall, shopping,
Clothing swerts Mineskert high heels	t-shirt, shorts, blouse, Dress, boots, shoe, sandels sneakers, Dress shoes
Transportation	car, boat, bike, Moto, motorcycle Plaing, bus, truck,
Everyday chores/tasks Cooking do the laundry Baby-sitting Make the bed	Cleand the house, room, wash dinishes, moping they past the bathrom
Food /Cooking cooking Gay food made stove grill Restaunts toaster and Micowave MC Donals stove, oven,	rice, beans, chiken, pork Duck, turkey Pizza, hamburger, soup, hot dogs
Crops/ Animals	cows, chikens, turkey dog, cat Duck
Furniture	soft chairs and sofa, Glass table
Tools and Equipment	computers, hammer tv, game, radio, cd, wash machiand telephone, dishwasher
Education	school and house home school colleges, high school university

inside them. Students were asked to finish the worksheet at home. One student's completed worksheet is shown.

- Students looked at the two worksheets they had filled out—one for the video about a colonial farm, and the other for present-day Maryland—and told me what they thought about life in Maryland now. Was it the same as in colonial times, or very different? There were no surprises here, as all the students could easily see how much life had changed. This became the first sentence of our essay, which I wrote on the blackboard: "Life has changed greatly in Maryland since the 18th century."

- I modeled a prewriting web on the blackboard. Students suggested categories where they saw the most striking differences, and I took notes around our topic sentence. As I did this, the students copied the web in their notebooks. When it was finished, I asked them to circle the three categories they found most interesting and would like to write about in their essay.

- Using the prewriting worksheet shown, I taught students to write the introduction, the body, and the conclusion of their essays. First, they copied

Students living in our suburban community did not know about crops and animals in present-day Maryland. When I teach this unit again, I will take students to the computer lab to research what crops our state specializes in. This activity can be modified for use with any community or state. The categories on the worksheet can also be changed or expanded.

Prewriting Worksheet

Name _____

Date _____

Now and Then

INTRODUCTION: (Write what you are going to prove in your essay, and list at least three supporting details you are going to use to prove your point.)

BODY

PARAGRAPH 1:
Topic Sentence (Write the first supporting detail.)

Examples (Give examples from your graphic organizer.)

PARAGRAPH 2:
Topic Sentence (Write the second supporting detail.)

Examples

PARAGRAPH 3:
Topic Sentence (Write the third supporting detail.)

Examples

CONCLUSION (Write what you think about the changes and/or paraphrase the introductory sentence of your paper.

---

our topic sentence; then they wrote which three elements of a community they were going to compare in their composition. Next, I explained that each paragraph of the body would be about one of the elements they compared.

- After a minilesson on paragraph writing, students wrote a topic sentence for each paragraph of the body of their essays. Their homework was to finish this part of the essay by adding supporting details. In class we discussed several ways to approach the conclusion, and students chose whether they wanted to paraphrase the introduction, express personal opinions on the changes, or do both.

- Over the course of several days the various stages of **process writing** were completed: writing the first draft, revising, editing, writing the second draft, and publishing. Some of the students included computer graphics in their essays. One student's completed essay is shown.

Structured worksheets help students with limited educational background approach difficult writing tasks such as a compare and contrast essay. Even the weakest students are able to complete this assignment successfully following the prewriting format. In every class there are one or two gifted writers who tend to be more creative and go beyond the frame of the structured writing. I try to use these creative writers as an example to teach students how they can make any piece of writing personal and original.

ASSESSMENT

Students used a checklist and the rubric shown for self-assessment. I used the rubric to grade the papers and to plan a minilesson on grammar. To ensure that every student would be successful in completing this assignment, the rubric included evaluation of all the steps of the writing process and only those elements of grammar that were specifically noted during the editing step. Students who did not meet the requirements of the rubric were invited to come for help during lunch or after school.

Language Minilessons

I believe that the best way to teach grammar is in a context that is meaningful to the students. Every time we have a project or an assignment, I carefully analyze what my students need to know and whether they already know it or not. What they do not know I address in language minilessons. For this particular assignment, all students needed instruction on the simple past tense and regular and irregular verbs, and most were unsure about capitalization rules and end punctuation. These three areas of grammar were the focus of the minilessons.

Completed Essay

Sadia Haque
11-20-98
pd.2
Ms.Ryzhikov

NOW AND THAN

Life has changed greatly in Maryland since the 18th century. Shelter/ building, tools and equipment, and education are not the same now as they were 200 years ago.

The first example of change is Shelter/ Building. In the18th century they had different shelter/building form now. In that time their house was made of logs and stones and now they made houses of wood and brick. In that time their kitchen and bathroom was separite from the house and now we live in single house, town house, apartments,skyscraper. And bathroom and kitchen are inside the house.

The second example of change is tools and equipment. In 18th century they had different tools and equipment from now. In that time they used hammer, axe and chisel and now they use hammer, and knife too. But they use computer, telephone, redio and Screwdriver too.

The third example of change is education. In the18th century they didn't have any education system. They learned at home with thier parents how to count. But now we have to go to school, high school , college and go home and do your homework with parents. And we have to learn many things not just counting.

I thing about changes are good for all of us, because now it is easire than 200 years ago. That time they had to do all the things along and now we can get help from many things, like from computer and teacher.

Rubric

Student: _____ Class: _____

Now and Then

1: Minimal　　　　　　2: Satisfactory　　　　　　3: Excellent

Writing Process

_____ Prewriting (two graphic organizers)

_____ Draft(s)

_____ Editing

_____ Revising

_____ Meets deadline

_____ (Total/15)

Content

_____ The introduction states the topic and lists all the supporting details that will be used in the paper.

_____ Each paragraph starts with the topic sentence.

_____ Each paragraph has at least two examples supporting the topic sentence.

_____ There are AT LEAST three paragraphs explaining the difference between Maryland "then" and "now."

_____ Connecting words are used correctly.

_____ The conclusion paraphrases the introduction and/or gives the writer's opinion on the facts presented in the paper (the writer says what he or she thinks about the change).

_____ (Total/18)

Mechanics

_____ Correct manuscript form

_____ Correct use of capitalization

_____ Correct use of end punctuation

_____ Correct use of the simple past and present tenses

_____ Correct paragraphing

_____ (Total/15)

_____ (Self-evaluation/2)

_____ (Final Total/50)

Grading scale		
45 – 50	=	A
40 – 44	=	B
35 – 39	=	C
30 – 34	=	D
0 – 29	=	E

Goal 1, Standard 3   To use English to communicate in social settings: Students will use learning strategies to extend their communicative competence.

Descriptors

- testing hypotheses about language
- exploring alternative ways of saying things
- self-monitoring and self-evaluating language development
- using the primary language for clarification
- using context to construct meaning

Progress Indicators

- test appropriate use of new vocabulary, phrases, and structures
- keep individual notes for language learning
- practice recently learned language by teaching a peer

PROCEDURE

- The first minilesson was on verbs. I asked the students to translate two sentences: *We play basketball every week* and *We played basketball yesterday*. Students had to find the verbs in their own language, highlight them, and tell me whether they were the same or different in both sentences. This was my bridge to the English verbs. I wrote two sentences with a regular verb (in simple present and past) and two with an irregular verb. Students had to tell me how the verbs in each set of sentences changed when we spoke about the past. After explaining the difference between regular and irregular verbs and distributing lists of the most commonly used irregular verbs, I asked students to highlight all the verbs they had used in the first drafts of their essays.

- Students worked in groups to create lists of the regular and irregular verbs they needed for their essays. Whenever they wrote something and were in doubt about a verb, they could consult their lists.

- Students then had to edit all the verbs in their first drafts to make sure their essays were in the past tense. This was done first individually, then with a partner.

- Our next minilesson was on capitalization. Students read a short paragraph about Asia from their ESL textbook, *All Star English*

All students in my intermediate class needed instruction in the simple past tense; however, the level of difficulty of the instruction varied for different students. Those with good academic backgrounds in their native languages had no problems transferring skills from one language to the other and were able to edit their own papers. Those with limited educational background had to first learn how to identify verbs because the concept was new to them. These students received extra help from me and from other students who had finished their editing.

(Richard-Amato, Abbot Hanson, Skidmore, & Drayton, 1997). In each sentence they had to look for the capitalized word and explain why it was capitalized. We then formulated two simple rules for capitalization: Capitalize the first word of every sentence and capitalize names. Students were then asked to read their essays, underlining the first word of each sentence and underlining names, and then checking to make sure they were capitalized.

Assessment

For all the written assignments in the unit, I monitored grammar through the rubrics. Students used checklists and techniques such as highlighting the verbs in their writing drafts to focus their attention on the verb tenses and capitalization.

Interdisciplinary Connections

Making connections between different disciplines in school is especially crucial for ESOL students. So instead of researching any community of their choice, my students made a connection with their social and world studies classes. Doing this helped students acquire the vocabulary necessary to be able to participate in their mainstream classes, taught them strategies to attack textbooks and supplementary materials used by mainstream teachers, and exposed them to the content of their mainstream classes—but on their own level of language development.

Goal 2, Standard 2   To use English to achieve academically in all content areas: Students will use English to obtain, process, construct, and provide subject matter information in spoken and written form.

Descriptors

- listening to, speaking, reading, and writing about subject matter information
- gathering information orally and in writing
- selecting, connecting, and retelling information
- analyzing, synthesizing, and inferring from information
- demonstrating knowledge through application in a variety of contexts

Progress Indicators

- take notes
- synthesize, analyze, and evaluate information
- locate information appropriate to the assignment
- record observations
- define, compare, and classify objects

Procedure

- The activity began in the media center with a minilesson on how to use the computer card catalogue to look for research materials. The students then worked by grade level to locate materials. All the sixth graders were studying Egypt at that time. They typed in the word *Egypt* to find all the materials available on this topic. Seventh graders did the same for the Renaissance Period in Italy, and eighth graders did searches for the Maya, Inca, and Aztec civilizations. Using their printouts, students located books, CD-ROMs, and videos on their topics.

- Students continued looking for information and taking notes on another copy of the same worksheet we had used from the beginning of the unit. They were encouraged to add any additional categories they thought were necessary and appropriate to describe their communities. Some of their suggestions, such as religion, government, and money, were excellent. I tried to make sure that all students had an opportunity to work with computer programs, videos if possible, and printed material. When they finished with one source, they started working with another.

- Meeting with students from each grade separately, I taught them how to work with a grade-level textbook. I had asked all the social and world studies teachers to give me copies of the textbooks and supplementary materials they used in their classes. We reviewed how to use the table of contents and the index. Concentrating on the pictures, chapter titles, headings, and subtitles, we predicted what kind of information we could get from the book and whether we could use it for our research. I modeled how to look for new vocabulary written in bold type and how to find explanations of the new terms in the text itself.

- Some of the mainstream teachers gave me notes from the lectures they used in their classes. I adapted them and, working with one group at a time, gave them the same information in easier language. Students were extremely attentive. All of a sudden things made sense!

- When students had collected information about all the different elements of their communities, they wrote down what sources they had used for their research and chose three elements about which they had interesting information. They would use this information for their next writing assignment: a letter about an imaginary visit to the community they had researched.

ASSESSMENT

The completed community worksheet allowed me to assess achievement of the progress indicators. I also used a checklist to evaluate which sources of information students used successfully and which sources were more difficult. Grade-level textbooks were definitely difficult for them. Some of them just copied sentences from the book without understanding their meaning. This led to additional discussions on issues such as plagiarism and the importance of paraphrasing the information in their own words. Students also worked in pairs to assess whether each of them had collected enough information to write a letter about the community they had researched.

Writing a Letter

This was the second major writing assignment of the unit. I wanted my students to learn how to read a writing prompt and try a new form of writing: a friendly letter. In the letter, students had to describe an imaginary trip back in time to a community they had researched. This gave them the opportunity to summarize the research they had done and to write about community with a creative slant.

Goal 2, Standard 2   To use English to achieve academically in all content areas: Students will use English to obtain, process, construct, and provide subject matter information in spoken and written form.

Descriptors

- retelling information
- selecting, connecting, and explaining information
- responding to the work of peers

Progress Indicators

- synthesize, analyze, and evaluate information
- locate information appropriate to the assignment
- edit and revise own written assignments

Goal 3, Standard 1   To use English in socially and culturally appropriate ways: Students will use the appropriate language variety, register, and genre according to audience, purpose, and setting.

Descriptor

- using a variety of writing styles appropriate for different audiences, purposes, and settings

Progress Indicator

- write a letter using appropriate language forms

PROCEDURE

- After I gave students the writing prompt (see p. 135) and asked them to read it, they had to "unlock" it—figure out what the form, the audience, the topic, and the purpose of their writing would be. After recording this information, they had to find in the prompt the information that had to be included in the content of their letters. They wrote it down on a sheet of paper that had been folded in fourths, with one section used for each requirement.

- I used a short minilesson to show students the form of a friendly letter. We discussed its parts (address, date, salutation, body, closure, and signature), and I placed a poster with the same information in the room for quick reference.

- Students listed their ideas for the letter on the prewriting sheet where they had written the four requirements. Homework that day was to write a first draft of the beginning of the letter, explaining how the writer reached the ancient land.

Narrative Prompt

Imagine that you have been transported by a time machine into ancient lands. Write a letter to a friend about what life is like in the land you are visiting and how you feel about it.

Before you write, think about how your journey started. Also think about what you saw in the land. This may include shelter, clothing, food, transportation, tools and equipment, education, religion, everyday chores and tasks. Also think if life in the land that you are visiting is easier or more difficult than in present day Maryland and why.

Now, write a letter to a friend about what life is like in an ancient land and how you feel about it.

Narrative Prompt

FORM _____

AUDIENCE _____

TOPIC _____

PURPOSE _____

- In class the next day students shared their work, reading the beginnings of their letters and commenting on each other's work. This was a valuable activity, especially for students whose prior schooling did not stress creativity. Listening to their classmates and the models provided helped these students feel much more confident about approaching this assignment, and they were able to add to their beginnings, revise them, or change them completely.

- During the next several days students completed their letters using all the steps of the writing process. I taught a minilesson on conferencing, modeled a writing conference with one of the students, and then asked students to work in pairs and follow the steps on the conference worksheet below.

- It was for this assignment that Wei invented the wonderful Journey Train that took her to the magic book

This assignment can be easily adapted to differing interests and language proficiency levels. Instead of traveling to the past, students can be asked to travel to the future and imagine how life in their communities will be different at the end of the 21st century. Lower proficiency students could be allowed to write about only one interesting thing they "saw" in the ancient land. Another option is to allow students to draw and label pictures of what they saw.

Conference Worksheet

MY JOURNEY TO THE PAST
A Friendly Letter

Writer's Name _____

Conference Partner _____

Date _____

Content:

1. How does the writer explain his or her journey to the past? (Explain in one or two sentences.)

2. What elements of the community does the writer talk about in his or her letter?
   a.
   b.
   c.
   d.
   e.

3. What does the writer think about life in the ancient land?

4. What did you like the best in the letter?

5. What advice can you give to the writer?

Mechanics:

1. Is the first word of every sentence capitalized?

2. Are all the names capitalized?

3. Is the story written in the past tense? (Highlight all the verbs.)

4. How many paragraphs are there in the letter?

5. Is every paragraph indented?

6. Does the writer follow the friendly letter format?

Friendly Letter

Gaithersburg, MD
208777
DECEMBER 10, 1998

Dear Sandeep,

One day in the morning when I woke up I saw my mom and she gave me a magic ring and the ring had a button and it was a beautiful ring, and she said if I push the botton I will get in ancient Egypt. When I got to Egypt I saw mummies.

When I got to Egypt I learned about mummies. A mummy was made out of dead body. The Egyptians believed that life on earth was only a part of an individuals total lift. After an earthly death a person was believed to come back after when they die. The people took out their liver, intestines, stomach, human head and place it into an conopic jar.

When I got to Egypt; I saw some beautiful building, some of those building were build by the Egyptians. They were made out of stone, mud bricks, and soil from the river banks.

In Egypt during the ancient time Egyptian men preferred short skirts, and their women wore long tight dresses of pleated linen. They also made all kinds of cosmetics from ground up minerals including red iron oxide; black galena; blue malachite. It was not just for women- men wore cosmetics and fine jewelry too.

During my visit in Egypt I ate dinner with the Egyptians they had all kinds of food some their food was Beastly Bread, and of the drinks they had wine, and beer. They cooked in an open fire place they also had fruit; some of their fruit were figs grapes, and pomegranates.

The things that the Egyptians used for furniture: brick platforms, chair, beds, and table. The things were covered with animals skins.

When I was in Egypt I started my way to school. The Egyptians boys and girls started school the age of five and completed it at 16 or 17, from the age of 13 or 14, boys were given special training they could enter a temple college and train to become a priest or a scribe in school they learned science, medicine and mathematics.

Your friend,

Vashti Smith.

where she had to make her choice. Wei was a seventh grader who was studying Renaissance Italy in her world studies class at that time. Vashti, a sixth grader, talks about traveling to Egypt in the friendly letter on page 137.

Assessment

Students learned to assess their own work and their peers' work using the conference worksheet. Peer conferencing is a difficult task for a language learner, and I recorded in my journal whether students were able to ask clarifying questions, identify all necessary parts of a letter, single out elements of a community in their partner's work, and find mistakes in verb tense and capitalization.

As students were going through the writing process, I carefully observed areas where they needed help. When the letters were finished we published them and put them on display on our bulletin board. I also asked the world studies and social studies teachers to read them, write a short comment, and give students extra credit in their classes if possible. My students were excited about getting their papers back with their mainstream teachers' remarks, and I had an opportunity to evaluate the progress of ESOL students with my colleagues. Most of the teachers commented personally on how much they enjoyed reading the letters. These comments were extremely important for my students' self-esteem and feelings of achievement.

Exploring Community Values Through Folktales

Values are an important aspect of any community and are reflected in the folklore of the community. Reading American folktales with my students was one way of exploring community values. My students' peers have heard names such as Paul Bunyan, John Henry, and Johnny Appleseed at home or in school, but my students have not. This activity helps bridge that gap in my students' backgrounds, while at the same time providing exciting reading material to expand their vocabulary, improve their reading skills, and help them relate to the values of their new homeland.

Procedure

- To review the concept of value, I asked my students to look at their personal goal statements from the first unit of the year, Hopes and Dreams, where they had written what they valued most in life. Together, we made a list of values words (e.g., *family, freedom, happiness, good work*).

- Students watched the video *The Legend of Johnny Appleseed* (Jackson, 1958), and I introduced the words *folktale* and *folk hero.* On their lists of values words, I asked students to circle all the words that could apply to Johnny Appleseed. To check comprehension, I asked students to write in their journals the names of folk heroes from their countries and the values they stood for.

- I had in the classroom a collection of folktales adapted for ESOL students (Cameron, 1994). Students were asked to choose any folktale they wanted and read it with a partner. I guided them in their choices to ensure that they were sufficiently challenged but not overwhelmed. Each pair was responsible for presenting the folktale to the class later. To help students read the folktale and prepare the presentation, I gave them questions for guided reading (see p. 139). Each pair also had to draw pictures illustrating the main events in the story.

Goal 2 Standard 3 To use English academically in all content areas: Students will use appropriate learning strategies to construct and apply academic knowledge.

Descriptors

- applying basic reading comprehension skills such as skimming, scanning, previewing, and reviewing text
- using context to construct meaning
- taking notes to record important information and expand one's reading
- actively connecting new information to information previously learned
- recognizing the need for assistance and seeking it appropriately from others

Progress Indicators

- verbalize relationships between new information and information previously learned in another setting
- make pictures to check comprehension of a story
- skim headings, illustrations, and captions to determine the key points in the reading
- seek more knowledgeable others with whom to consult to advance understanding

ASSESSMENT

While students were reading and preparing to present their folktales, I moved around checking comprehension, and helping with the vocabulary and summary of the story. In my journal, next to the name of each student, I recorded the level of participation and

---

American Folktales

Title of the folktale:

Setting (when and where?)

The main character's name:

What did the main character look like? Find words describing him or her in the text.

What was a problem/conflict that the main character faced?

What character traits did he/she demonstrate while coping with the problem?

What value does he/she stand for?

---

the ability to guess the meaning of new words from context, infer information, draw conclusions, and give examples from the text.

Presentation of the Folktales

In order to expose my students to as many folktales as possible, I wanted them to share the ones they read with each other. Another goal of the presentations was to teach them how to speak in front of their classmates and keep the audience's attention. ESOL students often feel intimidated when they have to speak in front of their peers in their mainstream classes. These presentations provided an opportunity to practice their speaking skills.

Goal 3, Standard 2 To use English in socially and culturally appropriate ways: Students will use nonverbal communication appropriate to audience, purpose, and setting.

Descriptors

- demonstrating knowledge of acceptable nonverbal classroom behaviors
- using acceptable tone, volume, stress, and intonation

Progress Indicators

- maintain appropriate level of eye contact with audience while giving an oral presentation
- maintain appropriate body language during the presentation
- analyze nonverbal behavior

PROCEDURE

- We developed the rubric shown on page 141 for the presentation, discussing together the characteristics of a good speaker. Students mentioned voice, body language, fluency of speech, and of course the content. Role-playing a presentation, I held the paper in front of me, completely covering my face, and asked my students to comment. That provoked a lot of laughter.

- We then spoke about what makes it easy for listeners to understand the speaker and decided that every presentation should have a visual illustrating the folktale. Students were given time in class to prepare visuals, such as a poster or a transparency with the new words they were going to teach their classmates.

- During the presentations, the other students took notes about the folk heroes.

ASSESSMENT

I videotaped students' presentations so they would later have an opportunity to analyze their own performance. Their analysis focused on body language, eye contact, and tone of voice. To check their understanding of the concept of community values, I asked them

---

Rubric for Oral Presentation

Oral Presentation

   1- Satisfactory   2 - Good   3 - Excellent

Information

Speaker included in his/her presentation
- the setting of the folk tale
- the main character's appearance
- the problem/conflict of the story
- character traits supported by the examples from the tale
- values the main character stands for

_____/15

Visual

The speaker's

- visual includes the name of the folk hero
- visual includes the values he/she represents
- illustrations and writing are neat and easy to read
- visual helps the audience understand the tale

_____/12

Speaking Skills

The speaker

- uses an appropriate tone of voice
- clearly pronounces word endings
- speaks fluently and with expression
- makes eye contact with the audience
- uses body language that does not distract the audience

_____/15

TOTAL _____/42

---

to write in their journals reflections on the questions: "What values do American folk heroes stand for? Are these values still important in our community? Explain your answer. Give examples from the book(s) you have read individually. Do you know any modern heroes? What values do they stand for?"

Creating an Ideal Community

For the culminating activity of the unit, students put together all the skills and information they had learned and applied them to a new situation, creating their own ideal community.

Goal 2, Standard 2   To use English to achieve academically in all content areas: Students will use English to obtain, process, construct, and provide subject matter information in spoken and written form.

Descriptors

- retelling information
- selecting, connecting, and explaining information
- listening to, speaking, reading, and writing about subject matter information
- representing information visually
- demonstrating knowledge through application in a variety of contexts

Progress Indicators

- synthesize, analyze, and evaluate information
- gather and organize the appropriate materials needed to complete a task
- take a position and support it orally and/or in writing
- locate information appropriate to the assignment
- edit and revise own written assignments
- prepare and deliver a short persuasive presentation

Goal 3, Standard 1   To use English in socially and culturally appropriate ways: Students will use the appropriate language variety, register, and genre according to audience, purpose, and setting.

Descriptors

- using humor appropriately
- determining appropriate topics for interaction

Progress Indicators

- create a cartoon
- express humor through verbal and nonverbal means

PROCEDURE

- Students worked in pairs to create a slide show about an ideal community. Each pair invented a community, named it, and placed it anywhere in the world they wanted to. They were required to include a minimum of five elements of a community, but they were encouraged to be creative with the elements. They had to include both graphics and language in their slides, and record their voices giving a tour around their community.

- Students worked on their slide shows in the computer lab for several days. I monitored their progress and helped those who had problems coming up with creative ideas.

- On the day of the presentations everybody was excited. Students could not wait to show their slide presentations and see what their classmates had done. Together we traveled to an ideal community in space, where everybody had a small spaceship for transportation; to a remote island in the ocean, where nature was beautiful, the weather was perfect, and everybody valued peace, hard work, and family; and to a community in the mountains, where everybody had a computer, hard work was done by robots, and peace was the main value.

ASSESSMENT

Students were able to assess their own work as they developed it, using the rubric below, which listed the requirements of the assignment. I used the same rubric to evaluate their work.

Conclusion

Before we started a new unit, students completed a self-evaluation. They looked at the goals they had written at the beginning of the unit and evaluated their work. Where were they most successful? What could they do better? What would they like to achieve in the next unit?

Rubric for Ideal Community

Student _____   Class _____

Ideal Community

    1- Minimal   2- Satisfactory   3- Excellent

_____ Describes the setting of the community

_____ Describes the inhabitants (people who live in the community)

_____ Describes the types of shelter in the community

_____ Describes the clothing of the community

_____ Describes the food people eat in the community

_____ Describes values of the community (at least two)

_____ Describes an additional element of the community (student's choice)

_____ Uses correct spelling

_____ Uses recorded narrator's voice and/or sound effects

_____ Is colorful, creative/original

TOTAL _____ / 30

Portfolio Reflections

Portfolio Reflection: Reading

List all the reading you have done this semester.

Which one did you enjoy the most? Why?

Which reading did you find the most difficult? Why?

What are your goals in reading for the next semester?

Do you think that reading has helped you in learning English? Why?

Portfolio Reflection: Writing

List all the writing pieces you have completed this semester.

Which piece are you most proud of? Why?

Which writing did you find the most difficult?

What would you do differently on your next writing piece?

Because the end of this unit was also the end of the semester, students also reflected on their progress in reading and writing during the first half of the year (see above). Then we were ready to move on to our next theme.

REFERENCES AND RESOURCES

The accelerated reader computerized reading management program [Computer software]. (1998). Wisconsin Rapids, WI: Advantage Learning Systems.

Applied Optical Media Corporation. (1994). *Language discoveries* [CD-ROM]. West Chester, PA: Author.

Bowen, C. (Producer). (1993). *A colonial farm* [Video]. (Available from Historical Video Productions, PO Box 12173, Silver Spring, MD 20908)

Cameron, P. (1994). *Larger than life, folk heroes of the United States.* Englewood Cliffs, NJ: Prentice Hall Regents.

Daddone, M., Eisner, R., Rikhye, R., Rosen, L., Rucker, M., Ryzhikov, O., Sammarco, T., & Sprehn, L. (1998). *ESOL curriculum: Middle school intermediate level.* Rockville, MD: Montgomery County Public Schools.

Jackson, W. (Director). (1958). *The legend of Johnny Appleseed* [Video]. (Available from Coronet/ MTI Film and Video, 108 Wilmot Road, Deerfield, IL 60015)

Kemper, D., Meyer, V., & Sebranek, P. (1998). *All write.* Wilmington, MA: Great Source Education Group.

Microsoft ancient lands [CD-ROM]. (1994). Redmond, WA: Microsoft.

Raimes, A. (1983). *Techniques in teaching writing.* Oxford: Oxford University Press.

Richard-Amato, P., Abbot Hansen, W., Skidmore, C., & Drayton, A. (1997). *All star English: Student book 2.* Reading, MA: Addison Wesley.

Short, D. (2000). Using the ESL standards for curriculum development. In M.A. Snow (Ed.), *Implementing the ESL standards for pre-K–12 students through teacher education* (pp. 103–136). Alexandria, VA: TESOL.

TESOL. (1997). *ESL standards for pre-K–12 students.* Alexandria, VA: Author.

TESOL. (in press). *Scenarios for ESL standards-based assessment.* Alexandria, VA: Author.

UNIT 6
Discovering the Interdependency of Living Things: Earthworms

ROGER GEE

Introduction

My students and I have a garden that serves as the basis for many activities throughout the year: completing a grant application with a video, entering contests and speaking with judges, attending an awards ceremony, gathering seeds and flowers to dry, propagating plants from cuttings, making crafts for a holiday craft sale, growing plants from seeds, conducting a plant sale, helping kindergarten students plant marigolds around the flagpole, and keeping records of what we do.

We also work in the garden. We prepare beds, plant, water, fertilize, mulch, weed, and deadhead flowers. Of course, there is a good deal of talking involved as we learn about which flowers to grow or buy, decide where to put them, read the weather report to learn what days will have good working-in-the-garden weather, and negotiate who is going to do what job. All of this requires using language for many different functions.

As I work with my students, I know they are acquiring language, but in the past, I often had difficulty specifying just what language was being learned and why. When I did describe a specific feature, it did not sufficiently capture what actually occurred. For example, in the spring, my students kept daily work records of what they did in the garden. Because they wrote after working, it was quite natural to use the past tense. Studying the past tense sounded professional to my principal and me. Yet there was so much more: requesting the work form, pronouncing the names of unfamiliar plants, resolving spelling problems, and conferring with another student about what was written.

Context

Grade levels: Sixth, seventh, and eighth grades

English proficiency levels: Beginning–advanced

Native languages of students: Mixed; predominantly Spanish, Ukrainian, Liberian English

Focus of instruction: ESL/science

Type of class: Sheltered content

Length of unit: 3–4 weeks

ESL Standards for Pre-K–12 Students (TESOL, 1997) is useful in helping me describe what happens with the interplay of the garden and children's language. This unit will show how this occurs.

Unit Overview

I developed the idea for this unit as I read an article in *The New York Times* about earthworms (Peterson, 1999). Students often encounter earthworms in our school garden, and they never fail to be a source of interest. Thus, I decided to begin a study of earthworms.

As a class we read the article and developed a test based on the information in the article. After this group study to provide a shared background knowledge of earthworms, each student developed a question, located information to answer it, and wrote a page for a class booklet, *Everything (Almost) You Ever Wanted to Know About Earthworms.*

This unit follows a general plan I have for research projects. As a group, the class learns some basic knowledge about a topic of interest. Next, each student identifies an area for individual research, and then at the end, we come together as a group to finish up a project for the unit. This plan provides a framework for students to first acquire both content and linguistic knowledge about the topic and then pursue individual interests with the support of the others in the class.

This framework allows the students to take control of their own learning. I think that is important, and in the context of my class, it is necessary for two reasons. One is that there are three grade levels in the class, a wide range of language proficiency, and different academic backgrounds. Seldom is the same instruction best for everyone. A second reason is that we are not together as a group for the entire day. By grade level, the students leave my room for exploratory classes such as art and music. In addition, each student is also a member of one of six teams in the school, and some are mainstreamed into regular classes. These classes meet on a rotating schedule throughout the week, and the schedule may change if a team finds it necessary. So although we are able to do some work as a group in my class, students often undertake individual projects. The nature of the projects is adjusted to account for language and academic differences.

The unit overview shows the sequence of activities for the unit.

Standards

The ESL standards have been useful for me as I think about my students' language learning. In broad terms, I can say that my students are working toward the three goals: using language to communicate in social settings, to achieve academically in content areas, and to interact in socially and culturally appropriate ways. I know that as they work toward meeting these goals, they are working toward becoming proficient in English as a second language.

I also use the standards associated with each goal to describe more specific situations when our garden leads us outside the classroom. These contexts often provide opportunities for the students to progress toward meeting Goal 3: to use English in socially and culturally appropriate ways. For example, one Sunday in October, my students and I attended a garden contest award ceremony at an estate in upper Bucks County, Pennsylvania. The owner greeted each student in a receiving line as we entered. The students spoke with contest officials, went through a buffet, received an award, and when they went inside to use the bathroom, noticed that although it was a nice house

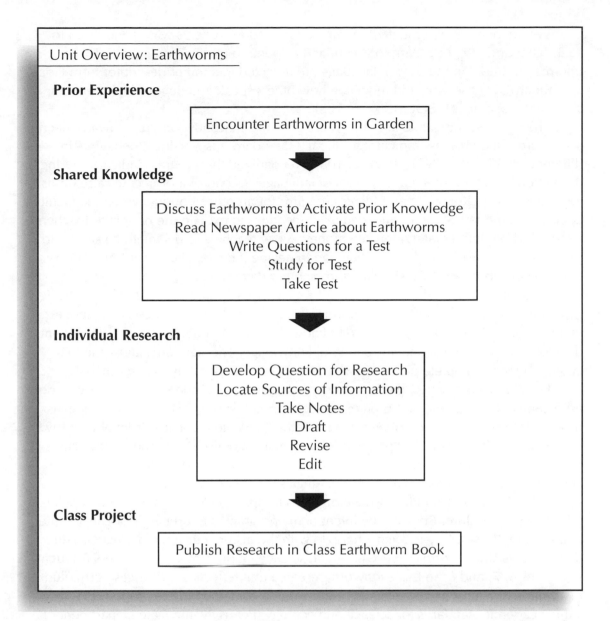

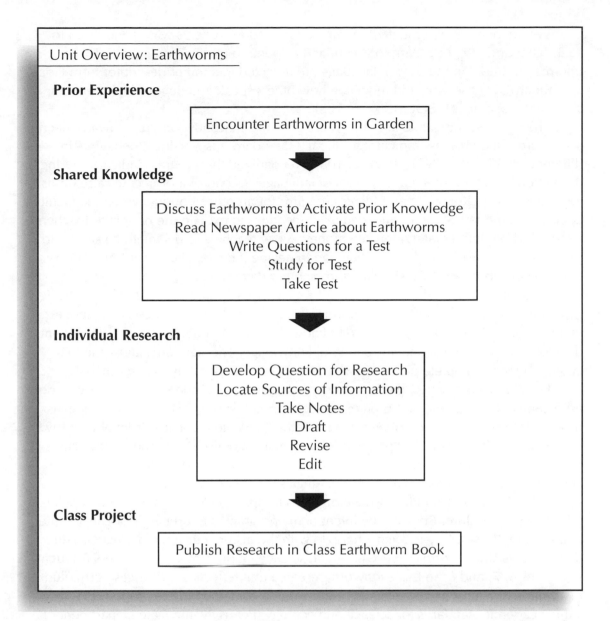

Unit Overview: Earthworms

Prior Experience

Encounter Earthworms in Garden

Shared Knowledge

Discuss Earthworms to Activate Prior Knowledge
Read Newspaper Article about Earthworms
Write Questions for a Test
Study for Test
Take Test

Individual Research

Develop Question for Research
Locate Sources of Information
Take Notes
Draft
Revise
Edit

Class Project

Publish Research in Class Earthworm Book

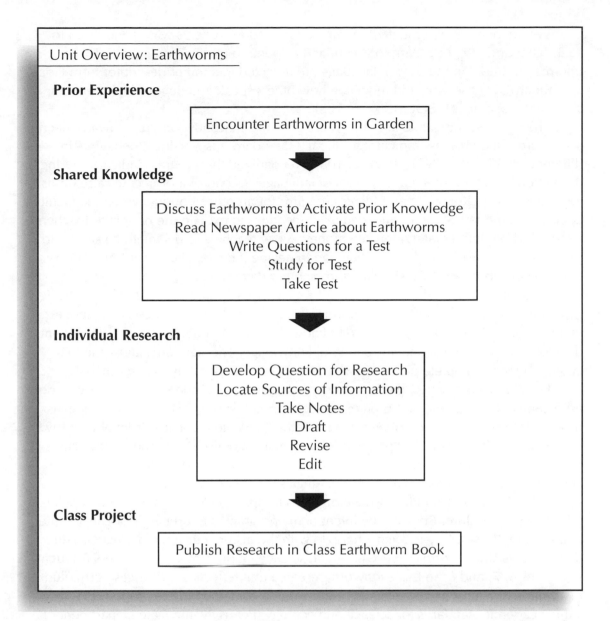

with 17 windows in front, there was no TV! As we returned from the party, I realized that my students had used English in socially and culturally appropriate ways.

As Goal 3, Standard 1 states, the students had used the appropriate language variety and register for that setting. The students had all been on their best behavior, and in the language of one of the descriptors, had used "the appropriate degree of formality" (TESOL, 1997, p. 95).

There are also out-of-classroom activities at school during which the students need to learn another set of cultural parameters, as work associated with our garden affords opportunities to use different registers of language. Goal 3, Standard 3 gives me a framework and language to describe what I do to prepare my students for these different situations; I am helping them "use appropriate learning strategies to extend their sociolinguistic and sociocultural competence" (TESOL, 1997, p. 103). A descriptor for that standard is "rehearsing variations of language use in different social and academic settings" (p. 103). That's a perfect description of what happens as we practice replacing the everyday language of our classroom with a more formal register to interview the principal for our garden grant video.

We are often complimented on our garden, and as students watch and listen to each other and me, they learn to accept and respond to these compliments. These informal and unplanned uses of language are reflected in another descriptor from Goal 3, Standard 3: "observing and modeling how others speak and behave in a particular situation or setting" (TESOL, 1997, p. 103).

The progress indicators are observable activities that show progress toward meeting a standard. One progress indicator for Goal 3, Standard 3 is "evaluate behaviors in different situations" (TESOL, 1997, p. 103). I recognized this progress indicator during a discussion about the social ambiguities of language. As part of a project to raise funds for refugees from Kosovo, the students cut tulips for an office bouquet when the faculty contributed money. Students attended team meetings to explain the project to teachers, some of whom immediately donated money. A few teachers said something similar to *I don't have any money today.* We then had to decide if the teacher meant *No, I don't want to contribute,* or if we should return another day.

Most of the planned activities for this unit address Goal 2: to use English to achieve academically in all content areas. Informal incidents such as those described above might go unnoticed but for Goal 3. Yet I know that such fortuitous events help students develop social language and sociocultural knowledge. The standards allow me to capture a more complete picture of what occurs in and out of my classroom.

For planned activities, the ESL standards serve as a reminder of what I need to do. I especially appreciate the inclusion of strategies for all three goals. To me a strategy is how to do something, and I often try to bring the "how" to a conscious level with my students. The descriptors and progress indicators that go along with the strategy standards are an excellent resource as they help me recognize what strategies students actually use and anticipate what other strategies would be helpful.

The standards also help me develop plans to link my ESL teaching to the regular education curriculum. Because the intent of my program is to prepare students to enter mainstream classes, I try to align what I do with the district curriculum. Regular education students study worms in seventh-grade science, and the research process is taught in Grades 6, 7, and 8, so this earthworm research unit reflects the district's curriculum. In addition, this unit meets several of the standards contained in the proposed Pennsylvania academic standards for science and ecology (Pennsylvania State Department of Education, 2000). As a result of this unit, students will

- explain biological diversity (Pennsylvania State Department of Education, 2000, p. 9)

- explain the flows of energy and matter from organism to organism within an ecosystem (Pennsylvania State Department of Education, 2000, p. 14)

- explain how species of living organisms adapt to their environment (Pennsylvania State Department of Education, 2000, p. 16)

The unit also addresses Pennsylvania's reading and language arts standards for first language students, which state that students will

- read and understand essential content of informational texts and documents in all academic areas (Pennsylvania State Department of Education, 2000, p. 4)

- use and understand a variety of media and evaluate the quality of material produced (Pennsylvania State Department of Education, 2000, p. 5)

- write multiparagraph informational pieces (Pennsylvania State Department of Education, 2000, p. 8)

I was therefore confident that the earthworm research unit approximated the education given to all students in my district. However, I was also aware that the unit was a weak version of what regular students experience. Yet I like to believe that I am providing a rigorous program for my students. This is where the ESL standards are especially useful. As noted in *ESL Standards* (TESOL, 1997), "The ESL standards provide the bridge to general education standards expected of all students in the United States" (p. 2).

The ESL standards operate on three levels for me. One is when I am beginning to plan. I review the standards, descriptors, and progress indicators as I anticipate how a unit will develop. At a second level, the standards help me respond to daily teaching situations that may be unanticipated even in planned instruction. Because of the student and institutional variables in my class, the day-to-day work of the students does not proceed in lockstep fashion. I also try to give students control over their learning so that they become independent and active learners. As a result, although we all work within the same general framework, each student's inquiry may involve unique learning needs and opportunities. Being familiar with the ESL goals, standards, descriptors, and progress indicators helps me recognize and respond to unanticipated situations. The third level is that of assessment, where descriptors and progress indicators give me specific examples of what to look for as I check students' achievement of the standards. In short, the standards help me anticipate as I plan, respond to students' needs as I teach, and observe as I assess.

I am comfortable with the standards, both those of Pennsylvania and those of TESOL, because, in general, they reflect my beliefs about education and language learning. The ESL standards validate what I do; the descriptors and progress indicators reassure me that I am providing a sound linguistic and academic basis for my students. The standards also give me a metalanguage that makes it easier for me to write plans, evaluate students, and discuss students with other teachers and with parents.

For me, the standards are a not a mandate to add something on to what I already do. Instead, they "indicate more specifically what students should know and be able to do as a result of instruction" (TESOL, 1997, p. 15). The standards help me make note of what my students do as they become proficient in social language, academic language, and socially and culturally appropriate uses of language. Their clarity helps make me aware of the value of what happens in my class, gives me tools to describe this value for myself and for others, and helps me recognize areas of need.

Activities

There are five main activities in this unit. Although they are described separately, in reality they overlapped and flowed into each other.

1. Shared Knowledge: Discussing Earthworms to Activate Prior Experience

2. Shared Knowledge: Reading to Understand the Essential Content of a Newspaper Article

3. Shared Knowledge: Constructing, Studying for, and Taking a Test Based on the Newspaper Article

4. Individual Research: Developing and Answering a Research Question With a Piece of Informational Writing

5. Class Project: Publishing Research Papers in *Everything (Almost) You Ever Wanted to Know About Earthworms*

Discussing Earthworms to Activate Prior Experience

As the students work in our garden, they frequently find earthworms. They have different reactions, including saying "yuck," playing with them, and curiosity. When I saw the earthworm article, I realized that it could be the common basis for everyone to share in an earthworm research project. However, I knew the reading level would be difficult for most of my students.

To prepare the students to read the article, I wanted them to be able to connect it with what they already knew from their experiences in the garden. They could use this known information to help understand the new information in the article. Because of their vivid experiences in the garden, prior knowledge would be easy to activate with a discussion.

> **Goal 2, Standard 1**   To use English to achieve academically in all content areas: Students will use English to interact in the classroom.
>
> ### Descriptors
>
> - participating in group discussion
> - following oral and written directions, implicit and explicit
> - asking and answering questions
>
> ### Progress Indicators
>
> - join in a group response at the appropriate time
> - respond to a teacher's request for information

PROCEDURE

- The students' desks are arranged in two lines facing each other to form a long rectangle. At each end of the rectangle a desk faces in so that in essence the desks are arranged in the shape of a large table. I rarely sit at my teacher desk; usually, I sit at one of the student desks. With this arrangement it is easy for the students to help each other and for me to help them.

- I reminded students of the earthworms we often see in our garden and asked what they knew about them. When information was volunteered, I repeated what was said and wrote the information on a piece of paper so I would not forget:

  What we know about earthworms:

  Earthworms are reddish brown.

  They live in the ground.

  They feel soft.

  They move around when we dig them up.

  Some students are afraid of them.

  The worms have a thing around the middle.

  They are good for the garden.

- To wrap up the discussion, I read the list I had made and then gave out a worksheet. Students were asked to answer the first item: Write one thing you know about earthworms.

Assessment

For this activity, assessment was based on observing students' participation. I noted that a low proficiency sixth grader did not participate in the discussion. She did, however, use Spanish to hold a short conversation about *los gusanos* with another girl.

> A few words in Spanish as this student reached out for peer assistance allowed her to continue participating in the English class activity. Such use of the native language in an ESL class is normal for social reasons, acceptable for stylistic reasons, and beneficial for academic reasons.

Reading to Understand the Essential Content of a Newspaper Article

In my middle school, worms are included in the mainstream seventh-grade curriculum. I wanted my group of sixth, seventh, and eighth graders to have some knowledge of worms as well. I also wanted to undertake an intensive reading—a careful and detailed reading of a difficult text—in which I would model reading strategies for content area materials.

Most of the reading my students do is extensive reading—large amounts of reading to get a general understanding. However, I believe that intensive reading helps students develop strategies useful for reading difficult texts in the content areas. My more specific objectives were that the students recognize the logical organization of a text, use illustrations to understand a text, practice assessing a sufficient level of comprehension, and understand new words using context. I also wanted the students to construct a linguistic and content area knowledge base that would enable them to engage in a research project.

Goal 2, Standard 2 **To use English to achieve academically in all content areas: Students will use English to obtain, process, construct, and provide subject matter information in spoken and written form.**

Descriptors

- listening to, speaking, reading, and writing about subject matter information
- analyzing, synthesizing, and inferring from information
- formulating and asking questions

Progress Indicators

- participate in a discussion to construct meaning as a text is being read
- locate information appropriate to an assignment in text or reference materials
- generate questions concerning specific topics in a reading

Any teacher can easily duplicate the resources for this activity. Our basic materials were a newspaper article, a worksheet used as a guide to writing questions, and students accustomed to participating in a discussion about reading to construct meaning. The article I used was "A Fertilizer Machine Fueled by Dirt" (Peterson, 1999). However, any article connected to the curriculum that is of interest to both the teacher and students may be used. The questions worksheet for this unit is shown below. It asks students to write questions based on information found in a specific paragraph or group of paragraphs in the article.

My rationale for a worksheet on which students write the questions follows.

1. The worksheet makes students aware of subtopics in a newspaper article. The topic of the article in this unit was earthworms, but there were a number of subtopics: mating, fecal matter, number and types of earthworms, and so forth.

2. To write a question, the students must locate the paragraph containing appropriate information in the article. This is an important reading strategy that Chamot (1999) calls *selective attention.*

3. The students may then use the language of the paragraph to help write a question. This is another strategy I teach my students. The text they read is a linguistic resource for writing.

4. Instead of responding to a text-based question written by me, the students have greater control over their own learning.

5. The questions written by the students are used in a test constructed by the group. Writing their own questions for a test helps students understand the

---

Questions Worksheet

Name _____ Date _____

Answer Question 1. Then listen to the article about earthworms. Ask questions about anything you don't understand. Finally, use the newspaper article to write questions about earthworms.

1. Write one thing you know about earthworms.
2. Write one question about earthworms and water.
3. Write one question about why earthworms are beneficial.
4. Write one question about how many earthworms are in a garden. (Sixth graders may want to write a ratio.)
5. Write one question about earthworms in North America.
6. Write one question about types of earthworms.
7. Write one question about getting earthworms in our garden.
8. Write one question about animals that eat earthworms.
9. Write one thing you would like to learn about earthworms.
10. How can you find an answer for your question?

Sample Think Aloud

As I began reading the article, I commented, "Hey, this begins like a story, not a science book." After reading a sentence in which the author comments on something she used to think, I said, "'She wrote, 'used to think.' She used to think that the rain flooded their burrows, their homes, so the worms came up to the surface and drowned in the water on the sidewalk. That's what she used to think, that they expired, they died. But it sounds to me like now she doesn't believe the worms die. Let's read some more and see." I later confirmed that prediction: "Yup, I was right; she learned that the worms can live under water; she used to think they died, but now she's learned they don't."

An expression used in the article, *make whoopee,* elicited this comment (from me): "The worms come up on the sidewalk when it rains to make whoopee; they look for mates. Mates are like girlfriends and boyfriends. I think *make whoopee* means something like they have baby earthworms. Let's read some more." A few sentences later my prediction was confirmed: "She wrote, 'enhance my population of earthworms.' That means to get more earthworms, so I think that's what *make whoopee* means, to find a mate to get more earthworms."

types of questions found on tests: short answer, multiple choice, and true and false. The students, of course, must be able to answer their questions.

PROCEDURE

- I explained that I had brought copies of an interesting article in *The New York Times* ("A Fertilizer Machine Fueled by Dirt," Peterson, 1999) that had a lot of information about earthworms. After the students paired up to share copies of the article, we looked at the illustrations. I pointed out the picture of the *burrow,* as it was an important word.

- I began to read aloud. Anytime I read aloud to students, I have two concerns. One, I need to mediate the text to make it comprehensible to the students. Sometimes this involves changing the language, stopping and explaining, and of course responding to students' questions. My second concern is to **think aloud** to model the habits and processes of a proficient reader. In the examples, my comments emphasize the style of the article, the *used to* construction, and prediction strategies; other parts of

My students, in addition to ranging from sixth to eighth grade, have a range of English proficiency and literacy levels. Given this situation, it is necessary to accept that some students will have less comprehension than others will after the first reading. However, by using the text as a basis for our inquiry, all students will understand the content and structure of the article as they work with me and with each other. In addition, they will continue to grow in academic language proficiency through continued interactions with the text.

the think aloud modeled connecting prior experience with the article and the use of indirect and direct context clues.

- As I continued in this fashion I also noted the changes in topics:

    1. the writer's experiences with earthworms
    2. some of the benefits of earthworms in a garden
    3. the amount of fertilizer produced by earthworms in a typical garden
    4. origins of earthworms in North America
    5. types of earthworms
    6. how to increase the number of earthworms in a garden
    7. dangers to earthworms
    8. a summary

Completed Worksheet

Karla Soto
Name

5/28/99
Date

Answer question number one. Then listen to the article about earthworms. Ask questions about anything you don't understand. Finally, use the newspaper article to write questions about earthworms.

1. Write one thing you know about earthworms.

   I knew that earthworms live under ground.

2. Write one question about earthworms and water.

   How long can earthworms live in water?

3. Write one question about why earthworms are beneficial.

   T or F   Earthworms are beneficial for the gardens because it make the plants grow bigger. (T)

4. Write one question about how many earthworms are in a garden. (Sixth graders may want to write a ratio.)

   About how many earthworms are in a back yard garden?

5. Write one question about earthworms in North America.

   T or F   There are 3 types of earthworms in North America. (T)

6. Write one question about types of earthworms.

   How many types of · earthworms are in South America?

7. Write one question about getting earthworms in our garden.

   Name something that we use last year for our garden, that the earthworms like.

8. Write one question about animals that eat earthworms.

   Name at least 2 types of animals that eats earthworms.

9. Write one thing you would like to learn about earthworms.

   I would like to know which earthworms are female and which ones are male.

10. How can you find an answer for your question?

    By looking on the internet or some kind of books.

- After we had read and discussed the article, students wrote questions as directed on the worksheet. One student's completed worksheet is shown.

ASSESSMENT

Worksheet Items 2–8 were used for assessment of this activity. The criteria:

1. Questions were directed at the specified topic.

2. Questions could be answered from the text or by using the text and prior knowledge.

3. Questions used conventional spelling and punctuation.

Worksheet Items 9 and 10 were also completed at this time. The worksheets were not simply collected and graded. As described in the next activity, the questions were used to construct a test, and the students worked with me and each other to decide if they had written "good" questions for a test. Questions that were not "good" were revised. This assessment was therefore a learning activity, especially for those students whose initial comprehension of the text was incomplete.

Constructing, Studying for, and Taking a Test Based on the Newspaper Article

As pointed out above, these activities were not discrete; they really flowed into each other. An advantage of this was that as students finished an activity, I was able to work with them for evaluation and to prepare them to move on to the next activity. As students completed the earthworm worksheet, we worked together to choose questions for the earthworm test.

This activity may be considered an adaptation of the usual routine of teach-review-test. After I chose the overall topic—earthworms—and helped students access a difficult text, the students were in control. They wrote the questions, took an active role in constructing the test, and had a copy of the test to study. Through this process, the students did indeed learn content and academic strategies, and they both learned and acquired language.

Goal 2, Standard 1 To use English to achieve academically in all content areas: Students will use English to interact in the classroom.

Descriptors

- expressing likes, dislikes, and needs
- elaborating and extending other people's ideas and words
- negotiating and managing interaction to accomplish tasks

Progress Indicators

- express a preference for including or not including a question on a test
- suggest revisions to questions in either form or content

Goal 2, Standard 2   To use English to achieve academically in all content areas: Students will use English to obtain, process, construct, and provide subject matter information in spoken and written form.

Descriptors

- understanding and producing technical vocabulary and text features according to content area
- persuading, arguing, negotiating, evaluating, and justifying
- formulating and asking questions

Progress Indicators

- revise and edit questions for a test using appropriate conventions
- answer questions on a test using appropriate vocabulary and sentence structure

Goal 2, Standard 3   To use English to achieve academically in all content areas: Students will use appropriate learning strategies to construct and apply academic knowledge.

Descriptors

- evaluating one's own success in a completed learning task
- applying self-monitoring and self-correction strategies to build and expand a knowledge base

Progress Indicators

- decide when to take a test after completing a sufficient amount of studying to ensure success
- rehearse and visualize information

PROCEDURE

- The students came to me as I sat at a computer. I worked with them to check their questions for content and conventions. The students had been working in pairs or groups, and this evaluation was usually a cooperative teaching activity as well.
- The first thing we looked at was content. Did the question address the topic? Was it a "good" question that could be answered from the text or a combination of the text and our prior knowledge?
- Then we looked at conventions. We had begun with a complete text, then moved to sentence level, and we were getting ready to publish the students' work in the form of a science test. For my students and me, this was the time to focus on form. Students asked themselves and each other questions such as:

Does each question start with a capital letter?

If needed, does each question end with a question mark?

Have we tried to spell each word correctly?

- We shared the questions to see if they sounded right, and, where necessary, I pointed out features for correction.

- After we decided that a student had developed a useful set of questions, the questions were entered into the computer to construct the test.

- For each question written by a student, I asked, "Is this a good question for our test?" This gave students the opportunity once again to have some control over their learning. It was also an opportunity for students to express likes and dislikes, to find questions that were redundant, and to discuss the demands of the question.

- Finally, the test was complete. As a group we decided when we would be ready to take it. Each student was given a copy, and students worked in study groups. All answers for the test, except for the true-and-false items, had to be in sentence form. I gave the students some strategies to help study for the test, with the hope of promoting interaction and language use as well as content area learning:

This negotiation over the content of the test was centered on information from the newspaper article. That written text—too difficult for the students to read independently—had been made accessible to them by an intensive reading of the text. By writing questions they had manipulated the language and content of the written text and were then engaged in conversation about the text. We began with the text and surrounded it with talking and writing, which provided opportunities for both language and content learning. This extra input surrounding a text is important for both low-proficiency and low-literacy students.

1. Work with a partner to find the answers.

2. Locate the appropriate paragraphs to find the answers.

3. Use the questions to help you write an answer.

4. When you have the answers, study with a partner.

ASSESSMENT

There were two types of assessment. I gave grades for the worksheet and the test. In addition to these teacher grades, the students engaged in self-assessment. Each student had to decide when to take the test. The students and I had agreed on a 2-day period for taking the test, and on one of those days each student had to determine when he or she had finished studying and was ready for the test. This self-assessment requires reflection that promotes independence as a learner.

I made one further adaptation. A beginning-proficiency sixth grader was concerned about having to write the answers in English. After much coaxing and consolation, on the afternoon of the last day for the test, she decided she was ready. She answered all of the questions in English, except for two. She asked to answer those last questions in Spanish. Of course, I agreed. She knew the content and had learned a considerable amount of English. Her completed test is shown.

Completed Earthworm Test

EARTHWORM TEST

Marcia   6/11/99
name   date

1. **Why are earthworms beneficial for gardens?**
   los gosanos acervollos y les entra aire alas plantas y las age creser.

2. **How many earthworms could be in our garden if it is 30 feet by 20 feet?**
   750 in our garden pf ptis 30 feet by 20 feet.

3. **How did earthworms come to North America?**
   Eathworms dio came to North American chos the Europ and the roots.

4. **How many types of earthworms are there in North America?**
   Ther are 3 types of earthworms.

5. **How can we get more earthworms in our garden?**
   We get more earthworms in garden by poting Organic meter.

6. **Name one bird that eats earthworms from gardens?**
   Robyn eats earthworms.

7. **How long can earthworms live in water?**
   Los gosanos duran en el agwa barias semanas.

8. **Why do earthworms come to the surface after rain?**
   Earthworms come to the sorface rain to mate.

9. **What are castings?**
   Castings are Fical meter.

10. **About how many earthworms are in 1 acre?**

   (A.) 53,000   B. 23,000   C. 53,000,000

continued on page 159

Developing and Answering a Research Question With a Piece of Informational Writing

The earthworm test was not the typical end-of-unit test, nor was it the end of the unit. Instead it was a way of consolidating a base of common knowledge and developing English language abilities to talk, read, and write about that knowledge. Publishing each student's informational writing in a class book was to be the culminating activity of the unit. The test was simply a step to prepare for this final activity. One objective for this unit was to add to our knowledge about earthworms, but more importantly, I wanted my students to practice using research and writing skills.

Completed Earthworm Test, *continued*

EARTHWORM TEST

11. Name 2 types of earthworms in North America.

The 2 types of earthworms are Night crawlers end Field worms.

12. What do earthworms like to eat from our garden?

Earthworms Kaie eat mulch

13. Name 2 animals, besides birds, that like to snack on worms.

Two animals that like to snack on worms mole and (Sorrillo < Skonk).

14. What do we put on our garden every year that the earthworms like?

We put mulch on our garden.

TRUE AND FALSE

15. _T_ Earthworms fertilize plants and help them grow bigger.

16. _F_ We have an acre in our garden.

17. _F_ Earthworms are not common in North America.

18. _T_ There are 3 types of earthworms.

19. _T_ Earthworms cultivate the soil.

20. _F_ Earthworms damage our garden.

21. _T_ Earthworms come to the surface to mate.

22. _F_ Skunks are the only animals that eat earthworms.

Informational writing is one of the three types or modes of writing specified in the Pennsylvania State Department of Education's (1999) *Academic Standards for Reading, Writing, Speaking, and Listening*, and report writing is also mandated by my school district's curriculum. At each grade level in the middle school, a content teacher and an English teacher team teach a research unit. The district asks students to develop research questions by first listing "What do I know?" and then "What do I want to know?" My school district also encourages the use of process writing. These state and district expectations fit very well with the ESL goal "to use English to achieve academically in all content areas" (TESOL, 1997, p. 9). The ESL standards are not an add-on for my program; rather, they help me organize what I need to do within the context of teaching at my middle school.

In general, this activity mirrors the course of the traditional writing process: prewriting activities, drafting, revising, editing, and publishing. More specifically, the activity follows my school district's steps for research papers: identifying a topic, activating prior knowledge, developing essential questions, and locating resources. On the worksheet for the newspaper article, students had written down one thing they would like to know about earthworms and then how they could find an answer for their question. They had noted a variety of resources: the library, a gardening encyclopedia we have in our classroom, electronic encyclopedias, a science teacher near our room whose students had studied worms, and, of course, the Internet. Then we began the actual research process.

I hesitate to recommend Web sites as things change so rapidly, but I will mention four sites that may be useful to anyone who wishes to replicate this unit. The City Naturalist site (1996) contains basic information about earthworms in a straightforward, not too difficult format. *The Burrow*, by Worm World (n.d.), has useful information on earthworm reproduction. "Worm World" was by far the favorite site of the students. "Earthworms" (n.d.) is a source for gardenless teachers to buy supplies to grow worms.

Goal 1, Standard 3   To use English to communicate in social settings: Students will use learning strategies to extend their communicative competence.

Descriptors

- seeking support and feedback from others
- focusing attention selectively
- self-monitoring and self-evaluating language development

Progress Indicators

- share a first draft for revision
- identify areas in which a classmate's first draft may be revised

---

Goal 2, Standard 2   To use English to achieve academically in all content areas: Students will use English to obtain, process, construct, and provide subject matter information in spoken and written form.

Descriptors

- listening to, speaking, reading, and writing about subject matter information
- formulating and asking questions
- gathering and evaluating information orally and in writing
- selecting, connecting, and explaining information
- responding to the work of peers
- analyzing, synthesizing, and inferring information

Progress Indicators

- locate reference materials
- locate and evaluate information appropriate to an assignment in text or reference materials
- select, organize, and synthesize information from multiple sources
- edit and revise written assignments

Goal 2, Standard 3   To use English to achieve academically in all content areas: Students will use appropriate learning strategies to construct and apply academic knowledge.

Descriptors

- focusing attention selectively
- applying basic reading skills such as skimming, scanning, previewing, and reviewing text
- recognizing the need for assistance and seeking it appropriately from others
- actively connecting new information to information previously learned

Progress Indicators

- scan several resources to determine the appropriateness to the topic of study
- scan an entry in a book to locate information for an assignment
- take notes to summarize the main material

PROCEDURE

- As students finished the test, we reviewed the questions and ideas for information on their worksheets, and the students set about gathering resources.
- As possible resources were located, students evaluated their usefulness. With books they looked in the index and table of contents to see on what pages appropriate information might be found. Then they scanned the text to see if it was really helpful. Some students knew how to use a scanning strategy for both print and electronic media. Others did not and needed to be taught. With all of the students, I modeled the strategy.
- After resources had been located, I reviewed the school district's bibliography cards and emphasized their usefulness. I pointed out that with

---

Bibliography Card

Name __Juan Carlos Salinas__   Bibliography Card No. __3__

Teacher __Dr. Gee__

Book

Author or Editor __Paul   F   Brandwein__ .
　　　　　　　　(Last)　　　　(First)　　　(Middle)

Title __Life__
　　　(Underlined)

City __New York__ : Publisher __Harcourt Brace__ and Woold , Date __1968__

Note Card

CENTENNIAL SCHOOLS   NOTE CARD

Life.

Name

Bib. # 344-345   Outline Key

Teacher, Period   Page(s)

Steps.

① Kill — place in Jar add water and chloroform.

② Strech out worm — Cork bord, foam, or Soft wood,

③ Pin down head, tail.

④ Not to deeply. Start at tail.

⑤ Pin back every 5 Segments.

One topic per card (in your own words). Don't forget page numbers.

the number of resources we had located, the bibliography cards would help the students remember where they had found information. At this time I also reviewed the district's note cards. A completed bibliography card and note card are shown.

- The students, my aide, and I worked together to locate and evaluate information and take useful notes that were legible and contained only information that would help answer the questions. There was a good deal of interaction as students helped each other and shared information.

- The next step was to organize and synthesize the information to write a first draft and enter it into a computer.

- As students completed a first draft, they knew that sharing their drafts in a peer conference would help them make their writing better. My students are trained to respond by phrasing their comments in one of three ways:

    1. *I like . . .* A specific feature or part must be mentioned. A general *I like it* gives little useful help.

    2. *I don't understand . . .* This comment can point out something that needs to be clarified.

    3. *I want to know more about . . .* In addition to helping the writer know where more information is necessary, it shows interest in what the writer has to say.

- Students' responses using the above framework tend to focus on the general content of a piece and are especially useful when the writing is shared aurally. I also helped the students revise and edit by using the ARMS acronym:

  A - add

  R - remove

  M - move

  S - substitute

  These responses to writing can focus on word-level concerns as well as larger units of language. For instance, it is possible to add or remove an article, move an indirect object, or substitute a compound word for a phrase. This revision and editing strategy is a bit more difficult for my students to use. I teach the ARMS acronym, but only the more proficient students are able to use it successfully and independently.

- After revision and editing were complete, the questions and answers were formatted for printing on "an earthworm page" to be included in *Everything (Almost) You Want to Know About Earthworms.* The students had to format their pages to follow the format guide shown, which we had all agreed on so that each page of the book would look the same.

ASSESSMENT

When students are doing a major piece of writing, I give several grades for the writing process. I use a grid to give a grade for topic selection, notes, first draft, sharing, and publishing. When a project is complete, the students fill out portfolio entry sheets and place the projects, including notes, drafts, revisions, and final copy, in their portfolios. At that time I enter grades into a computer-grading program. One student's completed portfolio entry sheet is shown.

A difficulty with this system is that I must enter a numerical grade into an electronic grade book, and it is often not easy to translate work done by students of different grade levels with a range of language and literacy proficiencies into equitable grades. Essentially, I give full credit (100 points) unless there is a reason not to. Although I am not entirely satisfied, I find that I can usually negotiate a reasonable grade with a student, especially as the work is a product of the interaction between the student and the rest of

---

Format Guide

This is how big to make your question.

Format your paper by using a Size 18 font for the question. Put it in the center. Then leave 4 spaces between the question and the answer.

When you write your answer, you need to make bigger margins. Make the left and right margins 2 inches. Make the font size 14. We will try to find a picture of an earthworm to put on each page. Each page will also have number. This way all of the pages in our book will look the same.

Completed Portfolio Entry Sheet

Portfolio Entry Sheet

Date _6/18/99_   Name _JuanCarlos Salinas_

Title of Piece:

➢ When did you begin work? _6/10/99_

➢ When did you finish work? _6/18/99_

What were the directions or purpose for this piece?

To Learn how to disect a worm.

Reflections

➢ Why are you putting this piece in your portfolio?

So I know how to disect a worm, these Shows that I know how to do research.

➢ Take a few minutes to think about your work on this piece and/or you plans for future reading or writing, and then write your reflections.

This will help Me remmember how to dissect a worm.
I Learned a science research and I Learned what materials, Procedure and observations mean.

the class, including myself. Furthermore, the ESL standards state that the progress indicators are not meant to "evaluate the quality of a student's performance or set benchmarks" (TESOL, 1997, p. 16). The standards also recognize that evaluation decisions may vary according to the students' backgrounds.

Publishing Research Papers

The culminating event of this unit was the publication of *Everything (Almost) You Ever Wanted to Know About Earthworms*. Publishing is a part of the writing process. It provides a reason for a focus on form and conventions: Someone else will be reading the research papers. In addition, the book will be a part of our classroom in the future. We can refer to the information. Equally important, it will help us develop a sense of community as we remember when we did this.

> ### Goal 1, Standard 1 To use English to communicate in social settings: Students will use English to participate in social interactions.
>
> #### Descriptors
> - sharing and requesting information
> - expressing needs, feelings, and ideas
> - engaging in conversations
> - conducting transactions
>
> #### Progress Indicators
> - ask peers for their opinions, preferences, and desires
> - engage listener's attention verbally or nonverbally
> - elicit information and ask clarification questions
> - clarify and restate information as needed
> - indicate interests, opinions, or preferences related to class projects

PROCEDURE

- Preparing the table of contents as the students finished editing helped the students visualize what they were working toward: publication. As the students' research neared completion, the titles of their pages became set, and we looked at the table of contents in several books to get ideas about formatting.

- After deciding how to format the page, the next step was to decide on organization. This was another opportunity to make the students aware of the logical organization of a text. The research was organized into three sections that included related topics. I used the computer to prepare the table of contents, but I did it in the classroom with the active participation of the students.

- A group of sixth graders designed a cover using word art in a word processing program. One student had a good deal of experience using word art and acted as the leader of the group. My students were able to work independently, but a few minutes of instruction should enable most students to use basic word art features. In addition to sharing and developing their abilities to use technology, the students were expressing feelings and ideas as they discussed artistic preferences.

- The seventh graders made a title page, which is shown. Together we looked at several books and noted the information on title pages: title, author, and publisher. They formatted the page and showed it to the rest of the class for approval.

Title Page

Everything (Almost) You Ever Wanted to Know about Earthworms

Log College Middle School
ESL Class

- Finally, the front cover and a back page were laminated, and the book was stapled along the left-hand side. We proudly showed our book to the librarian, and, to the students' delight, she ordered a copy for the school library!

ASSESSMENT

The content of the book that the students published had already been assessed in the previous activity, so the assessment of this activity focused on students' language use during interactions as they prepared the book for publication. I used an observation checklist to attempt to record students' achievement of the progress indicators. In addition to noting achievement in the use of English in social situations, the standards helped focus my attention on areas of need for those students who were not successful.

Table of Contents

Questions .... and Answers

Where earthworms live

The life of an earthworm

The body of an earthworm

Additional Information

Understanding the success of this unit requires some knowledge of the range and quality of the students' research. The table of contents for *Everything (Almost) You Ever Wanted to Know About Earthworms* serves to demonstrate this.

The range reflects the variety of interests the students chose to pursue after the class developed a shared knowledge of earthworms. The work done in this unit addressed the

---

Dissection Activity

Name _____ Date _____

HOW TO DISSECT A WORM

Materials
    sharp knife or razorblade
    20 pins
    foam board or piece of soft wood
    2 earth worms - large

Procedure
    1. Kill worm with 10% clorafin or 70% alcohol solution.
    2. Stretch out worm on foam board or piece of soft wood.
    3. Pin head and tail.
    4. Cut open along the upper mid line.
    5. Find these structures: pharynx, esophagus, heart, crop, gizzard, and
       intestine.

Observations

Conclusion

---

curriculum and content standards for our middle school, in addition to the ESL standards, and the unit helped prepare my students for entry into regular education classrooms.

I was particularly proud of the quality of the work by the student who wanted to
know how to dissect an earthworm. After reviewing the dissection procedure for earthworms and the format for writing up experiments in several science texts, he developed
a dissection activity for the class, which is shown. He asked his science teacher to lead
us in the dissection of an earthworm, and she agreed. Unfortunately, we ran out of time
to complete this and other follow-up activities in June. Over the summer I will check the
standards to help me finalize dissection plans for September.

RESOURCES AND REFERENCES

Classroom Resources

Bartholomew, R. B., & Tillery, B. W. (1984). *Heath earth science.* Lexington, MA: D.C. Heath.

Bradley, F. M., & Ellis, B. W. (Eds.). (1992). *Rodale's all new encyclopedia of organic gardening.*
    Emmaus, PA: Rodale Press.

Brandwein, P. F., Burnett, R. W., & Stollberg, R. (1968). *Life: Its forms and changes.* New York:
    Harcourt Brace & World.

Maton, A., Hopkins, J., Johnson, S., LaHart, D., Warner, M. Q., & Wright, J. D. (1997). *Parade of
    life: Animals.* Upper Saddle River, NJ: Prentice Hall.

McClure, S. (1993). *Rodale's successful organic gardening: Perennials.* Emmaus, PA: Rodale Press.

Microsoft Encarta Encyclopedia [CD-ROM]. (1997–1998). Redmond, WA: Microsoft.

Ramsey, W. L., Gabriel, L. A., McGuirk, J. F., Phillips, C. R., & Watenpaugh, F. M. (1986). *Life science.* New York: Holt, Rinehart & Winston.

Internet Resources

Day, L. (1996). (1996). Earthworms. *The City Naturalist.* New York: The 79th Street Boat Basin Flora and Fauna Society. Retrieved June 1, 1999, from the World Wide Web. http://www.nysite.com/nature/fauna/earthworm.htm.
   This site is a good primer for earthworm study as well as for other flora and fauna of New York City.

Earthworms. (n.d.). *Let's Get Growing!* Retrieved June 18, 1999, from the World Wide Web: http://www.letsgetgrowing.com/worms.html.
   This is a source for gardenless teachers to buy supplies to grow worms, as well as books and activity kits about worms.

Worm World. (n.d.) *The burrow.* Retrieved June 1, 1999, from the World Wide Web: http://gnv.fdt.net/~windle/.
   This site is hosted by Willy the Worm in "The Burrow." It has useful information on earthworm reproduction.

WormWorld. (n.d.). *The Yuckiest Site on the Internet.* Retrieved June 1, 1999, from the World Wide Web: http://www.yucky.com/worm/.
   This site features Wendell Worm, who does a clever "worm in the dirt interview" with his cousin Eddie the Earthworm.

References

Chamot, A. U. (1999, June). Learning strategy instruction in the English classroom. *The Language Teacher Online.* Retrieved July 15, 1999 from the World Wide Web: http://langue.hyper.chubu.ac.jp/jalt/pub/tlt/99/jun/chamot.html.

Pennsylvania State Department of Education. (1999). *Academic standards for reading, writing, speaking, and listening.* Retrieved March 22, 2000, from the World Wide Web: http://www.pde.psu.edu/standard/reading.pdf.

Pennsylvania State Department of Education. (2000). *Proposed academic standards for environment and ecology.* Retrieved March 22, 2000, from the World Wide Web: http://www.pde.psu.edu/standard/ecology.pdf.

Peterson, C. (1999, May 16). A fertilizer machine fueled by dirt. *The New York Times,* section 9, p. 6.

TESOL. (1997). *ESL standards for pre-K–12 students.* Alexandria, VA: Author.

Glossary of Techniques

Procedures often vary somewhat from teacher to teacher. The following descriptions represent one widely accepted variant, but implementation may change depending on the teacher and the context.

Big ideas/small details T-graph: A divided-page technique that helps students organize main ideas on one side and supporting details on the other. It helps students structure their paragraphs and ultimately write a five-paragraph essay.

- Ask students to fold a notebook page in half vertically.

- Ask students to first think about the two or three most important things that they learned from a lesson. These ideas are the "big ideas." The big ideas are recorded on the left side of the dividing fold, with a half page in between each idea.

- Ask the students to write three things about each big idea. These are the small details. Small details are recorded on the right side of the fold, across from the big idea. Depending on the activity and amount of detail, each of the small details could become a big idea, and more small details could be added.

- Discuss the structure of a paragraph with the students, pointing out main ideas and supporting details.

- Demonstrate how the organizer can be used to create a good paragraph.

- Later, extend this model, if desired, to show the structure for writing a five-paragraph essay.

Cloze reading passages: An assessment procedure in which words are omitted from a portion of the text. Although the original purpose of this fill-in-the-blank procedure was to test reading comprehension, the procedure is often modified for specific teaching purposes. The procedure for a classic cloze reading passage is as follows.

- Prepare a cloze passage by choosing a reading selection at the appropriate level. Leave the first two or three sentences of the passage complete. Then delete words at regular intervals, usually every fifth, sixth, or seventh word.

- Tell students to read the entire passage silently before filling in any blanks.

- After reading through the entire passage, have students fill in the blanks using context clues to guide their word choices.

In a modified cloze passage, random deletion is not used. Instead, words are selected for a specific teaching purpose, such as connecting a pronoun with its antecedent. The exercise can also take a multiple-choice format as students are given a choice of words from which to select. Students are still instructed to read the entire passage before filling in the blanks.

Dialogue cards: Index cards containing information that students will use to compose a conversation. This activity is often used as a warm-up at the beginning of class.

- Prepare pairs of index cards; they may be color-coded or numbered to identify speakers. Each card describes the situation and the student's role in the conversation. For example, one card might say that the student is a shopper in the mall who must find the shoe store. The other card might say that the student is a clerk in a store at the mall. The cards may also include a time reference. The situation may focus on a particular point of grammar or vocabulary usage. For example, the shopper might be instructed to ask the clerk five questions, using five different prepositions, to locate the shoe store.

- Give each pair of students a set of cards and a specified amount of time for oral preparation; they may not write down the dialogue. They then present the conversation orally.

Dyadic belt: A process whereby students interact with a number of different partners for a short period of time to accomplish a specific task.

- Divide the class into two lines, with pairs (or dyads) facing each other.

zzzzzzz

xxxxxxx

- Use an egg timer to mark 3-minute intervals. The paired students complete whatever is assigned—usually, but not always, some form of conversation or information exchange. At the end of the 3 minutes, all the xs move to their left, with the x at the far left circling around and going to the end of the x line. The process can continue until every x has spoken to every z, or can be stopped at any point.

- If there is an odd number of students, have one of them sit at the head of the line, like this:

zzzzzzz

x

xxxxxxx

- When it is time for the students to move, ask the x who is outside the belt to move to the far right of the x line, and the x nearest the "head" to move into that chair. The x at the head of the belt can either observe or be the timekeeper.

This device has many advantages. It helps students practice language and clarify thought. It gives the teacher an opportunity to sit back and have the students do the work. At the middle school level, another advantage is interpersonal: There is almost always a student whom classmates perceive at least temporarily as "difficult" or as an outsider. There are others who, at the moment, are sworn enemies. With the dyadic belt, all students are part of the activity. Those who do not get along need only interact (or sit silently) for 3 minutes, and then they move on. Occasionally, the interaction of the dyadic belt helps break down interpersonal barriers.

K-W-L-(H) chart: A chart used to help students access prior knowledge about a particular topic (What I *Know*), ask questions about the topic (What I *Want* to Know), and record what they learn (What I *Learned*). Some teachers add a fourth column for recording the way in which they learned (*How* I Learned). A K-W-L-(H) chart may be done by the class as a group, with the teacher recording the information on a large chart on the chalkboard or on poster paper. This technique is often used to record what students are learning throughout a unit.

- Introduce the topic and have students brainstorm what they already know about it. Record their ideas in the What I *Know* column.

- Ask students to think of things they would like to learn about the topic. Record their questions in the *Want* to Know column.

- Elicit suggestions for how they could learn the things they want to learn. As they later gather this information, write it in the What I *Learned* column. (Include the resources where the information was obtained in the *How* I Learned column.)

- Use the chart as a basis for planning instruction on this topic.

- Return to the chart periodically and add to it, filling in the *Learned* (and *How*) column(s) as students discover answers to any of the questions in the *Want* to Know column.

When students complete the chart individually as part of a lesson, it is an excellent way of assessing their comprehension of a concept and independent application of new strategies.

- On the day you begin a new lesson, give the students a three- or four-column sheet with K-W-L-(H) at the top.

- Introduce the topic and ask students to list anything they already know about it under the *K* column.

- Next, ask students to list the questions they have about the topic, under the *W* column.

- Teach the lesson.

- Ask students to fill in the last one or two columns after teaching your lesson (emphasizing that they should include in the last column not only the resources they encountered, but also any strategies they used).

Process writing: An approach to writing in which students explore a topic through writing, using prewriting activities, drafts, revising, and editing. This approach gives students time to explore new ideas and new language to express them, and provides feedback on the content of their drafts.

- Use a variety of prewriting activities to help students explore the topic: discussion, reading, graphic organizers, brainstorming, list making, and drawing.

- As students put their initial ideas on paper in a first draft, make sure they understand that they should be writing for content rather than perfect form.

- Help students use feedback from themselves, peers, and the teacher to revise the content. Develop a procedure in which students learn to look first for something they like in a peer's paper, and next comment on what could be improved. The first reader should respond only to content and not correct grammar or mechanics at this point.

- Have students write their second drafts, making changes based on the feedback.

- When revision of the content is finished, have students edit their writing for spelling, grammar, and mechanics. This can be done by the students themselves or with a partner.

- Have students publish and share it with an audience.

Running reading record: A system of notations for recording information while a student reads aloud. The notations are usually made on a form that includes the text the child is reading, the date it was read, and space for notations, but the information can be recorded on Post-it notes or other note cards and added to the running record.

- As the student reads aloud, record miscues by writing the original word and its miscue. A system of abbreviations can be used to indicate common miscues such as substitutions, omissions, or reversals.

- In a separate section of the record, note the student's strengths, such as reading a particularly difficult word, or reading a word the student had previously miscued.

- Use the records to plan individual instruction or focused small-group or class lessons.

Sentence strips: Strips of paper containing parts of a whole, for example, parts of a story or parts of a procedure. Students must read the strips and organize them so they make sense when put together. Generally these strips contain no sequence words, which would make putting them together an easier task.

- For sequence strips for a procedure, create a procedure for a task. The task may be one that is done in class, such as measuring a certain way, or at home, such as combing one's hair.

- Cut the procedure apart into separate strips of sentences. Give each student a strip.

- Ask students to share their strips and to organize the strips into a whole procedure again, in the correct sequence.

Sustained silent reading (SSR): A period of time that is set aside every day for students to read books of their own choice.

- Give students 10–15 minutes every day to do nothing but read.

- Suggest that they find a book in the class library if they do not already have something to read.

- Spend this time reading yourself.

Think aloud: A teaching strategy in which the teacher models the strategies of a good reader by verbalizing thoughts while reading.

- Choose a narrative or expository text.

- Decide what strategies you wish to model.

- As you read the text, use natural language to interject thoughts that model the strategies.

- Later, during formal, planned instruction, label the modeled strategies.

Unplanned think alouds do not focus on specific strategies, but model what an effective reader does during reading. The teacher may simply verbalize reactions to the text.

Venn diagram: A graphic organizer used to help students compare and contrast. It consists of two or more overlapping circles and can be used to compare two or more areas. It is very useful in assessing students' ability to compare and contrast and to help them focus their writing.

- Present the areas to be compared and contrasted from a previously read text or previously discussed subject.

- Brainstorm detailed characteristics to be compared and contrasted from these areas. For example, if you were comparing and contrasting two different characters in a story, you could list adjectives describing these characters. As the students brainstorm, list these characteristics to the side of the Venn diagram.

- Review the list of characteristics, and for each one, decide if it applies to only one of the things being compared or to more than one. Then write it in the appropriate area. For example, if only one character in the story was kind, that adjective would go in the circle designated for that character. If both characters were intelligent, that word would be placed in the overlapping section of the circles.

Word splash: A way of introducing a concept and the language that accompanies that concept. Students determine the relationship between words in a set they are given, a process that helps them think about the concept.

- Choose a vocabulary domain, or any part of a concept broken down into words.

- "Splash" the words all over the page, making sure there is no visible order.

- Ask students to determine the relationship among the words.

- Ask students to put the words in some organized form, based on a task such as a list, a story, or a laboratory procedure.

About the Editor and Writers

Barbara Agor, when she wrote this unit, was the sixth- to eighth-grade ESL teacher at the inner city Charlotte Middle School in Rochester, New York. She started in the profession as a Fulbright grantee to India and has since taught at every age level and in a variety of situations. She holds a BA, MA, and PhD from the University of Rochester and has worked in teacher education there, at State University of New York, Brockport, and currently at Nazareth College. She is chair of TESOL's Serial Publications Committee and the editor of the Grades 9–12 volume in this series.

Roger Gee is the sixth-, seventh-, and eighth-grade ESL teacher at the Log College Middle School in the Centennial School District in suburban Philadelphia, Pennsylvania. He has earned MA degrees in TESOL and in Spanish, and a PhD in reading and language arts. In addition to ensuring that his students meet the Pennsylvania standards for mainstream students, he teaches undergraduate and graduate courses in reading, language arts, and TESOL.

Suzanne Irujo, editor of this volume and this series, has taught ESL at all grade levels and spent many years teaching methodology and language acquisition courses and supervising ESL student teachers at Boston University. Her BA is in Spanish, her EdM is in bilingual education, and her EdD is in second language acquisition. She is semi-retired, dividing her time between consulting on and editing ESL-related projects and enjoying the New Hampshire woods.

Paula Merchant has worked as an interpreter and has taught adult ESL in community college, workplace, and higher education settings. After getting an MA and state certification in TESOL, she found herself working part-time as a K–12 ESL teacher at four schools in Dedham, Massachusetts. The program has grown so much that she is now a full-time ESL teacher in the middle school, where she has been instrumental in securing training for the mainstream teachers who work with ESL students. She is also developing a standards-based curriculum for ESOL students based on the state English language standards and TESOL's ESL standards. She is a past president of MATESOL.

Olga Ryzhikov taught English in Russia before coming to the United States. She holds a BA degree in English, German, and education from Herzen University, and an MA in instructional systems development and ESOL from the University of Maryland, Baltimore County. She now teaches the intermediate- and advanced-level ESOL students at Forest Oak Middle School in Montgomery County, Maryland. She is part of a team that is writing and piloting a new ESL curriculum based on the TESOL standards.

Susan Sillivan has been teaching for 22 years, first as a Spanish and social studies teacher, and then as an ESL teacher. She now works with ESOL students in the English Acquisition Program at the East Hills Middle School in Bethlehem, Pennsylvania. She spent most of the year prior to writing for this volume developing units that utilize TESOL's ESL standards to shadow the standards adopted by the Bethlehem Area School District.

Dorothy Taylor was a first- through sixth-grade ESL teacher in Fairfax County, Virginia, when she developed, taught, and wrote the unit included in this volume. She has since moved to Buffalo, New York, and is now teaching adults at the University of Buffalo's Educational Opportunity Center. Her previous experience includes earning an MA in TESOL from the University of Maryland, teaching children in Rochester and Boston, and teaching adults in Buffalo. Throughout all her moves, she has maintained her interest in second language literacy, particularly writing.

Louise Young is a mainstream sixth- and seventh-grade science teacher at Dedham Middle School in Dedham, Massachusetts. All the ESOL students in the school are placed with the same team of teachers, and she and the other members of her team have been trained in ESL techniques and in using TESOL's ESL standards as a bridge to the state standards. She and her colleague Paula Merchant team-teach science courses for ESOL and mainstream students, and they collaborated on the unit in this volume. She loves to write and is a published author of children's books.

Users' Guide

Volume and Unit

Grade Levels	Pre-K–2						3–5						6–8						9–12					
	1	2	3	4	5	6	1	2	3	4	5	6	1	2	3	4	5	6	1	2	3	4	5	6
Pre-K	X																							
Kindergarten		X	X																					
Grade 1			X	X																				
Grade 2			X	X	X	X																		
Grade 3			X					X		X	X													
Grade 4							X		X	X														
Grade 5							X					X								X				
Grade 6													X	X		X	X			X				
Grade 7															X		X	X		X				
Grade 8																X	X	X		X				
Grade 9																			X	X	X		X	X
Grade 10																			X	X	X		X	X
Grade 11																			X	X	X	X	X	X
Grade 12																			X	X		X	X	X

Language Proficiency Levels	Pre-K–2						3–5						6–8						9–12					
	1	2	3	4	5	6	1	2	3	4	5	6	1	2	3	4	5	6	1	2	3	4	5	6
Beginning	X	X	X	X	X			X	X				X	X	X		X			X				X
Intermediate	X	X		X	X	X	X	X		X	X	X	X	X	X	X	X	X	X	X	X	X	X	X
Advanced	X	X			X	X	X			X			X	X		X	X		X	X				X
Native Speaker	X	X			X	X	X								X									

Program Models	Pre-K–2						3–5						6–8						9–12					
	1	2	3	4	5	6	1	2	3	4	5	6	1	2	3	4	5	6	1	2	3	4	5	6
Pull-out ESL[1]			X	X				X	X	X	X	X	X											
Departmentalized ESL[2]							X								X	X						X	X	
Intensive English[3]																			X					
Sheltered English[4]																	X	X		X				X
Inclusion/Push-in ESL[5]		X			X																			
Team Teaching[6]													X						X					
Mainstream Class[7]	X			X			X						X											

Language and Content Areas	Pre-K–2						3–5						6–8						9–12					
	1	2	3	4	5	6	1	2	3	4	5	6	1	2	3	4	5	6	1	2	3	4	5	6
Basic Academic Skills	X	X	X	X																				
Listening and Speaking	X	X	X	X	X	X	X	X	X	X	X	X	X	X	X	X	X	X	X	X	X	X	X	X
Reading		X		X	X	X	X	X	X	X	X	X	X		X	X	X	X					X	X
Writing			X	X	X	X		X	X	X	X	X			X	X	X	X	X	X	X	X	X	X
Social Studies			X		X	X	X	X	X	X	X	X				X			X					X
Science		X		X								X	X	X		X				X				
Mathematics		X		X		X							X							X				

Standards	Pre-K–2						3–5						6–8						9–12					
	1	2	3	4	5	6	1	2	3	4	5	6	1	2	3	4	5	6	1	2	3	4	5	6
Goal 1, Standard 1	X	X		X	X	X	X		X		X		X		X		X		X					X
Goal 1, Standard 2	X	X	X		X	X			X				X		X	X			X	X				
Goal 1, Standard 3	X	X		X	X	X	X	X					X			X	X		X	X		X		X
Goal 2, Standard 1	X	X	X	X	X	X	X		X	X	X	X		X	X	X	X	X	X	X		X	X	X
Goal 2, Standard 2	X	X	X	X	X	X	X	X	X	X	X	X	X	X	X	X	X	X	X	X	X	X	X	X
Goal 2, Standard 3	X		X	X	X	X	X		X	X	X		X	X	X		X	X	X	X	X	X	X	X
Goal 3, Standard 1			X	X	X	X	X			X	X	X	X	X	X				X	X	X			X
Goal 3, Standard 2				X	X						X	X				X	X		X					X
Goal 3, Standard 3		X			X	X						X	X	X					X					

[1] ESOL students spend most of their time in a single classroom and are "pulled out" of that classroom for ESL.

[2] Students rotate from one class to another; the ESL class is one of many regularly scheduled classes at a particular time.

[3] The focus is on fast acquisition of language skills, whether in a pull-out, departmentalized, or self-contained class.

[4] ESOL students are taught English through or in conjunction with another subject, such as science or social studies.

[5] The ESL teacher goes into a mainstream class to work with students; activities may be separately or jointly planned and conducted.

[6] The ESL teacher and content or grade-level teacher are both responsible for the class.

[7] ESOL students are placed in a grade-level classroom with both native and nonnative speakers.

Teaching and Learning Strategies	Pre-K–2						3–5						6–8						9–12					
	1	2	3	4	5	6	1	2	3	4	5	6	1	2	3	4	5	6	1	2	3	4	5	6
Computer Skills		X					X			X	X	X				X	X	X	X			X		X
Cooperative Learning				X	X					X	X				X	X			X		X			X
Critical Thinking				X						X						X				X				X
Independent Research		X						X			X		X			X	X	X						X
Literature	X	X	X	X		X	X			X										X		X		
Learning Styles	X	X		X	X			X					X	X										
Parent Involvement	X		X		X		X																	
Scientific Method			X												X						X			
Use of L1							X		X		X	X				X	X	X	X			X		X

Themes and Topics	Pre-K–2						3–5						6–8						9–12					
	1	2	3	4	5	6	1	2	3	4	5	6	1	2	3	4	5	6	1	2	3	4	5	6
Animals				X																				
Building Community								X																X
Careers		X	X																					
Colonial Life									X							X								
Communities, Helpers	X		X			X	X			X						X								
Environment											X						X							
Exploration														X										
Family	X		X					X															X	
Games									X															
Geography								X		X			X						X					
History								X	X				X			X			X					X
Measurement															X						X			
Multiculturalism		X		X	X	X	X	X		X	X									X				
Native Americans				X			X																	
Nutrition		X																						
Religions, Values																	X		X					
Self	X				X		X			X													X	
Socialization	X	X								X														
Writing Genres								X								X	X					X	X	

Also Available From TESOL

American Quilt: A Reference Book on American Culture
Irina Zhukova and Maria Lebedko

Common Threads of Practice:
Teaching English to Children Around the World
Katharine Davies Samway and Denise McKeon, Editors

ESL Standards for Pre-K–12 Students
TESOL

Implementing the ESL Standards for Pre-K–12 Students
Through Teacher Education
Marguerite Ann Snow, Editor

New Ways in Teaching English at the Secondary Level
Deborah J. Short, Editor

New Ways in Teaching Young Children
Linda Schinke-Llano and Rebecca Rauff, Editors

New Ways in Using Authentic Materials in the Classroom
Ruth E. Larimer and Leigh Schleicher, Editors

New Ways in Using Communicative Games in Language Teaching
Nikhat Shameem and Makhan Tickoo, Editors

New Ways of Classroom Assessment
James Dean Brown, Editor

Reading and Writing in More Than One Language:
Lessons for Teachers
Elizabeth Franklin, Editor

Teacher Education
Karen E. Johnson, Editor

Teaching in Action: Case Studies From Second Language Classrooms
Jack C. Richards, Editor

Training Others to Use the ESL Standards:
A Professional Developmental Manual
Deborah J. Short, Emily L. Gómez, Nancy Cloud, Anne Katz,
Margo Gottlieb, Margaret Malone

For more information, contact
Teachers of English to Speakers of Other Languages, Inc.
700 South Washington Street, Suite 200
Alexandria, Virginia 22314 USA
Tel 703-836-0774 • Fax 703-836-6447 • publications@tesol.org • http://www.tesol.org/